The Devil Kissed Her

The Devil Kissed Her

The Story of Mary Lamb

Kathy Watson

Jeremy P. Tarcher/Penguin
a member of
Penguin Group (USA) Inc.
New York

JEREMY P. TARCHER/PENGUIN
Published by the Penguin Group
Penguin Group (USA) Inc., 375 Hudson Street, New York, New York 10014, USA
Penguin Group (Canada), 10 Alcorn Avenue, Toronto, Ontario, Canada M4V
3B2 (a division of Pearson Penguin Canada Inc.)
Penguin Books Ltd, 80 Strand, London WC2R 0RL, England
Penguin Ireland, 25 St Stephen's Green, Dublin 2, Ireland (a division of Penguin
Books Ltd)
Penguin Group (Australia), 250 Camberwell Road, Camberwell, Victoria 3124,
Australia (a division of Pearson Australia Group Pty Ltd)
Penguin Books India Pvt Ltd, 11 Community Centre, Panchsheel Park,
New Delhi–100 017, India
Penguin Group (NZ), Cnr Airborne and Rosedale Roads, Albany, Auckland,
New Zealand (a division of Pearson New Zealand Ltd)
Penguin Books (South Africa) (Pty) Ltd, 24 Sturdee Avenue, Rosebank,
Johannesburg 2196, South Africa

Penguin Books Ltd, Registered Offices: 80 Strand, London WC2R 0RL, England

Jeremy P. Tarcher/Penguin
a member of Penguin Group (USA) Inc.
375 Hudson Street
New York, NY 10014
www.penguin.com

First Jeremy P. Tarcher edition 2004
First published in the United Kingdom in 2004 by Bloomsbury Publishing Plc

Most Tarcher/Penguin books are available at special quantity discounts for bulk purchase for sales promotions, premiums, fund-raising, and educational needs. Special books or book excerpts also can be created to fit specific needs. For details, write Penguin Group (USA) Inc. Special Markets, 375 Hudson Street, New York, NY 10014.

An application has been submitted to register this book with the
Library of Congress.

ISBN 1-58542-356-4

Printed in the United States of America
10   9   8   7   6   5   4   3   2   1

This book is printed on acid-free paper. ∞

Contents

Introduction

I had a sister
The devil kissed her
And raised a blister
Charles Lamb

O N THE AFTERNOON OF 22 September 1796, Mary Lamb killed her mother. She stabbed her at home, in the dining room, with the carving knife the family used at mealtimes, making this a homely crime as well as a violent one. Mary was thirty-one years old and, at the moment she raised the knife, quite mad. She had experienced mental illness before but, on that day, she had, in common parlance, lost her mind. She literally didn't know what she was doing. At that time, the Lamb household included herself, her paralysed mother, her dotty aunt, her father who was rapidly succumbing to senile dementia and her brother who had recently had a nervous breakdown. The family, therefore, was no stranger to eccentric, even extreme behaviour but Mary's act of matricide, one of the most rare of crimes, was beyond anything they had known before. For Mary, that single violent act was to change and determine the course of her life: she became one of those unfortunate people for whom biology is destiny.

Had Mary lived today, she would almost certainly have been diagnosed as suffering from a mood disorder. The nature of her illness – episodic with periods of normality interspersed with dramatic highs and lows – is the classic pattern of what British psychiatrists call manic-depressive illness and their American counterparts bipolar disorder. If she'd lived today, she could have benefited from the incredible amount of information that doctors now have on the nature, prognosis and outcome of manic depression. They would have been able to tell her that she was suffering from a neurological disorder, a disease that disrupted the normal chemistry of the brain. She would have been told that her illness was genetic – which accounted, no doubt for her brother Charles's breakdown – and that it affected between 1 and 2 per cent of the population. An episode could be triggered by sleeplessness, stress, an intense period of hard work or it could come out of the blue, seizing her swiftly and launching her, without warning, on a cycle that would begin with a mild high, spiral dizzyingly up into full-blown mania and then crash down into depression. The manic state might involve both pleasurable elation and total frenzy and the periods of depression might sometimes be so bleak that she would be a suicide risk.

Had she lived today, Mary would have been told that it was possible to manage her condition with at least one, possibly more psychotropic – i.e. acting on the mind – drug. Her prescription might include tranquillisers or anti-depressants; it would almost certainly involve lithium. Found in trace elements mined from rocks, lithium carbonate – a substance with a molecular structure of two atoms of lithium, one atom of carbonate, three atoms of oxygen – is believed to compensate for what is missing from the brain chemistry of people who suffer from manic-depressive illness. Its widespread use dates from the 1960s but ancient Greek and Roman physicians had long recommended that patients with 'nervous diseases' drink lithium water (water from springs with a high content of lithium). For some sufferers, lithium has been a lifesaver, reducing the highs of mania and easing the lows of depression. But lithium salts have a narrow therapeutic/toxic ratio and, if Mary was sitting in the consulting room of the psychiatric department of a modern hospital, she would be told about the possible side effects – drowsiness, muscle weakness, dizziness, blurred vision, ringing in the ears, nausea, weight gain, impaired speech, blackouts, chills, excessive perspiration and leg cramps. She might also have had therapy to help her understand her moods, to give her a place where she could vent her frustrations and ask for support as she came to terms with the diagnosis, the implications it had for her future and the reality of what it means to be on life-long medication. But Mary suffered from manic depression pre medication and before any thought of talking cures, and she and her family had to ride out the nightmare alone.

The magnitude of her crime, its violence and its terror, were breathtaking. But what happened next was no less extraordinary. Mary was not imprisoned or even punished in any way. Instead, she was set free to live with her younger brother Charles. For almost forty years, she shared his home, his friends and his literary career. Despite the awfulness of her crime, despite the recurring chaos of mental illness, with Charles's love and help, she created a happy, productive life for herself. Hers is a story of rehabilitation, of reconstruction on a grand scale.

Her life seethed with contradictions. The daughter who killed her own mother went on to write books for children, with *Tales from Shakespeare* being the best and most enduring; *The Swiss Family Robinson* is the only other children's book from that period still to be in print. She was self-educated, yet for a decade she presided over an informal literary salon that included the poets Coleridge and Wordsworth and the political thinkers Hazlitt and Godwin.

She was maternal but childless, domestic but unmarried. Most importantly, her illness caused her behaviour to swing unnervingly between the settled and the disordered. At regular intervals throughout her life, she was violent and dangerous and needed to be incarcerated in what her contemporaries bluntly referred to as madhouses. Her brother saw Mary's madness as separate from her, a cruel process by which she was lost to him and to herself. She was 'gone . . . her senses lock'd up and herself kept out', he once wrote and his first biographers adopted his view, seeing Mary's breakdowns as a piece of infernal bad luck that visited her every so often. 'I had a sister / The devil kissed her / And raised a blister' ran Charles's jokey triplet and her wildly changing moods, fierce, frequent and inescapable, must have seemed a devil's kiss indeed.

But Mary was ill, either manic or depressed, for several months of nearly every year of her adult life. To pretend the madness was a thing apart from her is not only to dodge the facts of her physical state but also to diminish the validity of the question that every biographer asks – what is this person really *like?*

The Ashmolean Museum in Oxford owns a Henry Fuseli print that may or may not be a portrait of Mary Lamb; the experts have yet to agree, perhaps they never will. The catalogue calls it 'Woman with a stiletto and a man with a startled expression'. In it, a crazed woman dressed in what looks like a nightdress holds up a thin knife. To the right of her head are the words Mary or Maria Anne and then what looks like an L. Is it Mary Lamb? In the Charles Lamb Society's archives, there exists a copy of another possible but disputed picture of

Mary Lamb. Here, the woman's black hair hangs down her back and the face is strong-willed and sensual. Is that Mary Lamb? It is unlikely that this portrait of a fashionable young woman with the flowers in her hair and the low-necked dress really shows Mary Lamb, who was a bluestocking with Unitarian principles and a radical outlook but there it is, in the archives, just in case.

The possibilities offered by these portraits are interesting. Is *that* my subject, is *that* what she was like? These are given an extra twist when asked of someone whose moods varied as wildly as Mary's. Which is the real Mary? Was she the quiet-voiced, well-read woman listening with intelligent interest to the opinions of the Lake poets, or the raging maenad with the knife? And what is the connection between the motherly lady who loved small children and wrote endearing and enduring stories for them and the terrifying creature so dangerous she needed to be put in a straitjacket? The truth is that she was both and her life – and the life of her brother – followed the contours of Mary's mental states, becoming a roller coaster of delight and despair, intimacy and separation, sweetness and terror.

There was no easy distinction between the two Marys. There was a mild-mannered Mary Lamb, a dearly loved sister and friend, a woman as gentle as her surname. And she inhabited the same body as another Mary, a frightening, irrational, violent one. There was a part of herself that Mary feared and mistrusted but she couldn't ignore. This is the story of how she came to terms with that part, how she reconciled the warring aspects of her personality and created for herself a whole and meaningful life.

Chapter 1

A Temple Childhood

That we had so much to struggle with, as we grew
up together, we have reason to be most thankful. It
strengthened and knit our compact closer
'Old China', Charles Lamb, 1821

ON 2 DECEMBER 1764, THREE weeks shy of Christmas, London was stunned and battered by freak thunderstorms. The following day Mary Lamb was born. She was her parents' third child. The first, a daughter, had died in infancy and the second, John, a strong healthy baby boy, had survived. Just eighteen months after his birth, Mary arrived.

She was born fairly and squarely into the servant class of Georgian England. In her father's background, there were gardeners and an owner of a grocer's shop but he had left the family home in Lincolnshire to go into service. John Lamb senior had been a footman in Bath and, at the time of Mary's birth, he was the personal servant to Samuel Salt, a childless, widowed barrister who lived alone in large, handsome chambers in the Inner Temple, the heart of the legal establishment.

Mary's mother Elizabeth had always been in service, being the daughter of the housekeeper at Blakesware, a mansion house in Hertfordshire owned by the Plumer family. Samuel

Salt was friendly with William Plumer, the county sheriff. Perhaps the gentleman's gentleman met the housekeeper's daughter on a visit to the country house and a relationship developed during the hunting and shooting season. Alternatively, they may have been introduced through Randal Norris, who was librarian and sub-treasurer at the Inner Temple and a good friend of John Lamb's. Norris's wife was born at Widford, near Blakesware and was a friend of Elizabeth Lamb's. Maybe a series of family gatherings brought together the London man and the village girl. However they met, what is definitely known is that, in 1761, they married at the church of St Dunstan's in the West, just outside the City of London, and set up home together beneath the chambers of Samuel Salt.

Salt lived well; he could enjoy the view over the Temple's handsome gardens and appreciate his chambers' fine panelling and fill his mahogany bookcases with books. And, to further ensure his comfort, below him, within easy call, lived his servant. John Lamb's quarters were smaller – two little rooms, in which he lived with his wife Elizabeth and his growing family. They shared their accommodation with their employer's wine collection. They also shared vicariously in the imposing grandeur of the Inner Temple. This majestic establishment, founded in the middle of the twelfth century by Knights of the Military Order of the Temple of Solomon in Jerusalem, was the centre of the legal profession, a place whose importance seemed embedded in its very architecture. It was made up of a series of handsome quadrangles, beautiful gardens, a dining room hung with coats of arms and a magnificent round church, modelled on the Holy Sepulchre in Jerusalem. Heraclius, Patriarch of Jerusalem, had consecrated the church in the presence of King Henry II and its interior had been fitted out by Sir Christopher Wren. Down the centuries, it had seen the dedication of medieval Knights Templars, the weddings of eminent MPs and the funerals of no less eminent lawyers, as well as the baptisms and burials of countless sad and forgotten foundlings, all given the name Temple. Into this hallowed and ancient building, baby Mary was carried, on 30 December, to be baptised. All around her were the ghosts of knights and lawyers; their effigies stood to attention, their names were carved into the walls and their bodies lay buried in a vault beneath the floor. There were more dead benchers – named after the long wooden trestles where they took their meals in hall – than live ones in the Temple.

Mary's father identified closely with the traditions of the Temple. As well as working for Samuel Salt, he also served as a pannierman, a robed waiter in the Inner Temple dining halls. There was money somewhere in his family – in later years, Charles Lamb talked of 'an old lady, a cousin of my father and aunts, a gentlewoman of fortune' – and he was relatively well educated. He was interested in literature, read the Whig paper, the *Guardian* and, in an age when it was unusual for even a member of the middle classes to own books, he possessed a copy of *Hudibras*, a seventeenth-century burlesque poem about Cromwell and the Presbyterian church written in Chaucerian couplets. In Bath, he'd been an active member of a friendly society – one of the many pre-Welfare State organ-isations that helped people on low incomes to save and provide themselves with a pension. He attended the society's weekly meetings, made speeches at them and recited poetry of his own composing at their dinners. His verses mingled wit and whimsy in equal measure. In 1770, he paid for a volume of his verse – *Poetical pieces on several occasions* – to be published. This slim volume included a sixteen-stanza saga about a chirping, dancing sparrow – 'a mighty bird for gallantry' – who gets married but prefers not to come home at nights: 'He spent whole days far from his home / There to each fair was vastly civil / and wish'd his wife safe at the devil.' There was also a cheerfully cynical rhyme about a widowed bullfinch who sets out to build a magnificent monument to her dead spouse, changes her mind at the last minute, remarries and very sensibly and promptly cancels the order to the stonemason. Perhaps John Lamb found married life and domesticity not entirely to his liking.

In appearance, John Lamb was square-faced and squarely built. His son, Charles who, as an adult, recast his father as Lovel and wrote of

John Lamb

a quick little fellow . . . a man of an incorrigible and losing honesty . . . the liveliest little fellow breathing, had a face as gay as Garrick's, whom he was said greatly to resemble, . . . possessed a fine turn for humorous poetry . . . moulded heads in clay or plaster of Paris to admiration, by the dint of a natural genius merely; turned cribbage boards, and such small cabinet toys, to perfection; took a hand at quadrille or bowls with equal facility; made punch better than any man of his degree in England; had the merriest quips and conceits; and was altogether as brimful of rogueries and inventions as you could desire.

Mary's mother, Elizabeth Lamb, was said to resemble the actress, Mrs Siddons. If that was true, then she was strong-featured with a long nose and dark hair and brows. A memoir of Mrs Siddons, written in 1782, stressed her energy and grace, her above-average height, her muscular frame and the fact that she carried herself in such a way that people thought she was more beautiful than she was.

At some point, John Lamb's sister, Mary's Aunt Hetty, joined the household. She was slightly eccentric, mixing her religious affiliations, poring over the Roman Catholic prayer book and Thomas à Kempis while firmly keeping the Sabbath Day holy at a Protestant church. She was responsible for the bulk of the housework while Elizabeth Lamb bore her children and helped her husband take care of Salt. The two women disliked each other. In later life, Mary recalled:

> My father had a sister lived with us, of course lived with my Mother her sister-in-law, they were in their different ways the best creatures in the world – but they set out wrong at first. They made each other miserable for full twenty years of their lives – my Mother was a perfect gentlewoman, my Aunty as unlike a gentlewoman as you can possibly imagine a good old woman to be, so that my dear Mother used to distress and weary her with incessant and unceasing attentions, and politeness to gain her affection. The old woman could not return this in kind, and did not know what to make of it – thought it all deceit, and used to hate my Mother with a bitter hatred, which of course was soon returned with interest.

This, Mary Lamb believed, was: 'the secret history' of 'all sisters-in-law' and, although she claimed that eventually, she and her brother: 'harmonised them a little' until 'they sincerely loved each other', twenty years is a long time to live amidst personal animosity and what we would now call class conflict. And although as an adult Mary described her aunt and mother's relationship frankly and with a clear-sighted lack of sentimentality, to a child, the atmosphere in the small apartment would frequently have seemed tense and unhappy.

As well as tension in the family, there was real tragedy. A year after Mary's arrival, her mother gave birth to a baby boy, Samuel, who lived only a month. Then, in September 1768, there came a little sister, Elizabeth. This child lived for five months before dying in the cold of February 1769. Mary was four, old enough to have known, held and loved the baby and the infant's death affected her deeply. Thirty years later, she could still remember her lost sister with pain and a clarity undiminished by time. She wrote movingly that 'the image of a little sister I once had comes as fresh into my mind as if I had seen her lately. A little cap with white satin ribbon, grown yellow with long keeping, and a lock of light hair, were the only relics left of her. The sight of them always brought her pretty, fair face to my view, that to this day I seem to have a perfect recollection of her features.' She must have shared her feelings of grief with Charles because, although he had been born after Elizabeth's death, he was none the less affected by her loss, once writing of 'A sister, I think, that should have been Elizabeth, died in both our infancies. What a comfort, or what a care, may I not have missed in her.'

The same year that baby Elizabeth died, her older brother John was sent away to boarding school, leaving Mary as the only child in the house. Two years later, her mother gave birth to Edward who lived only ten days. After that, there was a gap of four years – 'he was long a-coming,' Mary said – and then Charles was born on 10 February 1775. In her old age, Mary remembered her mother's pregnancy as a period of excited anticipation. She 'knew she had a little brother coming and was impatient to have him to nurse'. And when he arrived – 'this weakly but very pretty child' – she loved him.

The strain in Elizabeth's life, sharing a too-small home with a disliked sister-in-law, bearing seven children and losing four, affected her strongly. In particular, it seems to have stunted the affection she felt for her children. John was her favourite. He grew up to be a 'broad, burly, jovial, bulk', a robust child. With her experience of losing so many babies, she probably found his health and vigour delightful and reassuring. But Charles was small and weak with rickety legs and she was, frankly, mystified by Mary. When Charles created the character of Maria Howe in his story 'The Witch Aunt', he wrote of 'a weak and tender-spirited girl, subject to fears and depressions', a girl 'of a very different disposition' to her parents. He was describing his mother's impressions of both himself and Mary. According to Charles, his mother felt 'in opinion, in feeling, and sentiment, and disposition, so distant a resemblance to her daughter, that she never understood her right. Never could believe how much she loved her – but met her caresses, her protestations of filial affection, too frequently with coldness and repulse.' Her preference for John was unfair, she said; he 'was not worthy of one tenth of that affection, which Mary had a right to claim'.

Mary's father seems to have felt the same way. His *Poetical Pieces* included a verse entitled 'Letter from a Child to his Grandmother', in which he adopted the voice of his son, John.

> Dear Grandmam,
> Pray to God to bless
> Your Grandson dear with happiness;
> That as I do advance each Year,
> I may be taught my God to fear,
> My little frame from passion free,
> To Man's Estate, from Infancy;
> From vice that leads a youth aside,

And to have wisdom for my guide,
That I may neither lie, nor swear,
But in the path of Virtue steer,
My actions gen'rous, fair, and just,
Be always true unto my Trust;
And then the Lord will ever bless
Your Grandson dear
John L – b, the Less.

There were no poems on behalf of Mary and Charles. And Mary puzzled the grandmother addressed in the poem; her nervousness, her melancholy, the flashes of irrational thinking all bothered her mother. 'What are those poor crazy moyther'd brains of yours thinking of always?' she used to ask.

But the two overlooked children had each other. The gap – eleven years – meant that Mary was like a mother to Charles. She could carry him when he was a baby, hold his hand as he learned to walk, listen to him chatter, and comfort him when he hurt himself. Physically, they were alike; both were small with dark hair. Mary's eyes were brown while her brother's odd appearance was intensified by his different coloured eyes; one was brown, the other blue. 'Her smile was her brother's own,' said one friend. As often happens among people who are frequently together, their voices were similar. Charles had a pronounced stammer and Mary's voice was described by one friend as having 'a certain catch, or emotional breathingness, in her utterance . . . This slight check, with its yearning, eager effect in her voice, had something softenedly akin to her brother Charles's impediment of articulation.' Emotionally, they were even closer. The book of children's poetry they wrote together as adults avoided the usual (for the time) themes of nature and good behaviour and, instead, explored the theme of sibling love. Taken as a whole, the verses were a celebration of the strength and significance of a relationship between brother and sister. Parents made only brief appearances or were dead which reinforced the intimacy between brother and sister. 'I have got a new-born sister; / I was nigh the first that kiss'd her' runs Charles's poem 'Chusing a Name'.

> My parents sleep both in one grave
> My only friend's a brother.
> The dearest things upon the earth.
> We are to one another,

is the beginning of 'The Lame Brother'. There is the security of having an older sibling to look up to – 'Led by your little elder hand, I learn'd to walk alone,' continues 'The Lame Brother'. Poem after poem extols the pleasure of being an older child caring for a younger one. In 'Nursing', the child speaks:

> 'Oh, hush, my little baby brother;
> Sleep, my love, upon my knee,
> What though, dear child, we've lost our mother;
> That can never trouble thee.'

The final stanza reads:

> 'My only solace, only joy,
> Since the sad day I lost my mother,
> Is nursing her own Willy boy,
> My little orphan brother.'

There are poems in dialogue, conversations between brother and sister, arguments over toys, reconciliations and affirmations of lasting affection. They add up to a hymn of praise to the warmth of sibling love and the joy of sibling nurture, a relationship formed to compensate for the absence of parental interest.

The elder brother, John Lamb, was excluded – by age, by absence, by parental favouritism – from this intense relationship. It was a partnership of two, and as they grew so did their intimacy. Later Mary was to say that she and Charles shared a 'free communication of letters and opinions just as they arrive. . .the only groundwork of friendship'. And Charles was convinced that: 'close intercourse can only exist . . . in a family of two or three. In large families, 'the fraternal affection is ordinarily thin and weak'. The brothers and sisters can't 'get close enough to each other to share secrets and be friends'. They were both aware of and fascinated by the nature of their intimacy. Charles, in particular, attempted to describe it on several occasions: 'My sister indeed, is all I can wish in a companion,' he once wrote. However, there was a downside to this closeness. If one felt bad, the other soon did too; they reflected each other's ideas and thoughts in a way that could feel stifling. 'Our spirits are alike poorly,' wrote Charles, 'our reading and knowledge from the self-same sources, our communication with the scenes of the world alike narrow: never having kept separate company, or any 'company' together – never having read separate books, and few books together – what knowledge have we to convey to each other?'

The rarefied atmosphere of the Inner Temple reinforced their intimacy and intensified their sense of exclusion. An early eighteenth-century print of the Inner Temple gives a bird's eye view of its enclosed series of quadrangles, courtyards and gardens, the backs of the buildings turned away from the city. It was a self-contained, discrete world whose inhabitants lived according to their own rules and called their business meetings 'parliaments'; no one could be in any doubt that this was a kingdom all its own. They took their meals and their pleasures distinctively. The benchers had to dine in hall for a given

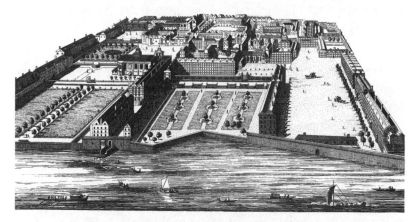

The Temple grounds.

number of times a year where they were called to table by the blowing of a horn and their meals served by a head porter dressed in an elaborate gown and carrying a bamboo staff topped with a silver Pegasus. Elaborate Christmas celebrations involved the lawyers treading a stately measure round the fire. The Inner Temple stood cheek by jowl with a notorious red light area but black-gowned, curly-wigged lawyers not prostitutes paced its famous rose garden where, according to Shakespeare, the Wars of the Roses began. There were more than 100,000 criminals in London but Mary Lamb lived among the men who tried their cases and made the country's laws. Popular legend claimed that Geoffrey Chaucer, that great storyteller, had been a clerk at the Inner Temple. Over one set of gates hovered two winged, stone Pegasuses as if to underline the place's mythical nature. The Temple had the inward-looking, hierarchical atmosphere associated with harems and, as First Waiter in the Inner Temple, Mary's father was part of its arcane mysteries. A contemporary record stated his duties clearly: 'First Waiter makes out the Bill of Fare, and lays it in the

Parliament Chamber every day in term time. As soon as the cloth is laid, serves up dinner for the first mess at the Bench Table, and in the absence of the Chief Cook attends the Gentlemen of the Bench after dinner to take orders for the Battlings and Exceedings for the next day; makes out the Cooks and Panniermen's bills on Calls to the Bar and collects the money for them.' There was an order to his daily activities, a structure to his service and a quaint and exclusive language used to signify the ordinary facts of eating and drinking and waiting at table. John Lamb and his children were familiar with the minutiae of this privileged, influential world but, as time was to make cruelly clear, they were ultimately not part of it.

And yet, for all its age, customs, legends and traditions, there was a newness about the Inner Temple. It may have had its roots in the past but many of the buildings had been recently built. The names were never changed, which created a sense of antiquity and continuity, but Crown Office Row, where the Lambs lived, was only thirty years old. It had been rebuilt in 1737, replacing another set of buildings that had been rebuilt in 1628. The Great Fire of 1666 had destroyed all the buildings in the King's Bench Walk. And although the architectural style might have suggested grave debate and quiet, contemplative counsel, the gardens ran down to the River Thames,

The house on Crown Office Row.

a river that was then a fast-moving major highway and its boatmen swept the lawyers and the MPs away to Westminster and to the courts where they made and enforced the country's laws.

It was usual to send children out of London to country relatives particularly during the summer months when the capital became hot, stinking and unhealthy. Mary spent part of every year in Hertfordshire either in the great house of Blakesware with her maternal grandmother, Mrs Field, or nearby on a farm in the village of Mackery End with Mrs Gladman, her mother's great-aunt. From a young age, Charles came too; on Mary's last visit when she was fourteen or fifteen, she had, she said, 'the care and sole management of him'.

Mrs Field had worked as housekeeper for the county sheriff and then, after 1767, for his widow, Elizabeth Plumer. When the widow died in 1778, the heir decided against living in Blakesware – it had been built in 1640 and he probably thought it old-fashioned – and went, instead, to live in another, newer property. Mrs Field was left at Blakesware as sole custodian of the house and grounds. Like Mary's father, her grandmother seems to have enjoyed her position as upper servant. Charles, in the poem 'The Grandame', wrote of her eating 'well-earned, the bread of service', and recalls 'with what a zeal she served her master's house'.

She might have been preoccupied with good servitude and, as the poem went on to stress, keenly aware of social position – 'Wise she was, / And wondrous skilled in genealogies, / And could in apt and voluble terms discourse / Of births, of titles, and alliances' – but, to young children who have yet to work out the world's pecking order, it must have been as if she were the real owner of this ancient imposing mansion with its many turrets, gables and carved chimneys. Perhaps, too, for those glorious summers, it was as if the children themselves owned it. Both Mary and Charles left their impressions of the house in their adult writing, impressions which are diamond bright with the intensity of their nostalgia. The young Margaret Green in Mary's short story 'The Young Mahometan' paces a large marble hall, hung with the heads of the twelve Caesars. There were Hogarths (when Mary was grown up and mistress of her own home, there were always Hogarth prints on the walls). There were 'carved chimney pieces', 'antique furniture' and 'curious old ornaments', tapestries and a library to browse in. Margaret Green is intimate with the details of the house. 'In another corner stood a marble figure of a satyr; every day I laid my hand on his shoulder to feel how cold he was.' It is a gesture both possessive and explorative. She feels a powerful affinity with the people in the family portraits on the wall: 'I used to long to have a fairy's power to call the children down from their frames with me. One little girl in particular who hung by the side of a glass door which opened into the garden, I often invited to walk there with me, but she still kept her station – one arm round a little lamb's neck, and in her hand a large bunch of roses.' And there was all the suggestive flotsam and jetsam of an abandoned house. 'An old broken battledore, and some shuttlecocks with most of the feathers missing . . . which constantly reminded me that there had once been younger inhabitants here' and there were mysteries, 'highly praised rarities' hidden from the child under an 'envious cloth'.

Blakesware spoke to Mary's imagination, and nearby Mackery End appealed equally strongly to her senses. For her story 'The Farmhouse' she drew on memories of visiting there, creating an artfully artless rendering of childish prattle as young Louisa Manners describes a visit she makes to her sister, Sarah, who, for some reason never explained, lived with her grandmother. Mary, a Londoner through and through, used the eyes of Louisa, another city child, to show us the beauties of the English countryside. There is an almost swooning sense of the place's loveliness. Louisa Manners overflows with her responses to the farm.

'There were pear-trees, and apple-trees, and cherry-trees, all in blossom,' she recalls. 'These blossoms were the prettiest flowers that ever were seen, and among the grass under the trees there grew butter-cups, and cowslips, and daffodils, and blue-bells. Sarah told me all their names, and she said I might pick as many of them as ever I pleased . . . I filled my lap with flowers. I filled my bosom with flowers, and I carried as many flowers as I could in both my hands.'

All nature conspires to make her happy. The grandmother says that a 'delicious syllabub' is 'a present from the red cow to me because it was my birthday; and then because it was the first of May, she ordered the syllabub to be placed under the Maybush that grew before the parlour door, and when we were seated on the grass round it, she helped me the very first to a large glass full of the syllabub, and wished me many happy returns of that day, and then she said I was myself the sweetest little May-blossom in the orchard.'

Everything about the story speaks of abundance and generosity, nature tamed and ordered by careful husbandry. There are baskets of flowers, ripe currants and gooseberries to pick, a 'nice clean dairy', with 'pans full of milk and cream', a crackling fire, an old shepherd, and bacon hanging under the chimney. It is the perfect English pastoral scene, painted by its artists, evoked by its poets and, here, rendered with all the bright, sensitive colours of childhood memories, blooming once more in the words of Mary Lamb.

But Mary, like Louisa, was a London child, a little Cockney. Both saw the greatest beauty in city streets. Lolling in the heart of her pastoral idyll, Louisa admits she likes the daisies best. 'I have even picked a daisy, though I knew it was the very worst flower of all, because it reminded me of London.' The crowds, the restlessness, the sounds of the big city have their own beauty. Louisa is fired up with excitement when she describes London, 'how the houses stood all close to each other; what a pretty noise the coaches made; and what a many people there were talking in the streets.' She playacts that she is back there and explains how London has made her self-assured. 'I obtained a great deal of praise . . . because I replied so prettily when I was spoken to. My sister was more shy than me; never having lived in London was the reason of that.' Another of Mary's young heroines, Emily Barton, also thrills to the music of London: 'the bustle and confusion of people . . . the crowded streets and the fine shops'.

Mary loved London and, during the years she grew up there, the capital was fizzing. It was renowned throughout Europe as a place where people knew how to enjoy themselves. Although it was possible, from the Inner Temple, to be walking in country lanes within fifteen minutes, the city none the less had an urban sensibility and energy. Just outside the gates of the Temple lay Fleet Street, the haunt of journalist and writers, packed tight with booksellers, and places to drink. The Devil Tavern had been Ben Jonson's favourite spot and Samuel Pepys had been fond of the Hercules Pillars. Alongside them stood places that did a brisk trade in quack medicine, selling drops for the palsy, cures for the plague, lozenges which supposedly cured consumption, and powders for toothache.

By day, the shopkeepers employed apprentices to stand in the street and shout: 'Buy, buy.' Women just in from the country shouted out the price of apples, flower girls proffered posies, chimney sweeps and knife grinders offered their services and the dancing bear performed to the sound of his master's drum. There were dancing girls, there were acrobats, there were men handing out advertisements for new plays. The noise was immense as the sellers cried out their wares and the wagons and coaches rumbled over the cobbled streets.

At night, Londoners partied in neighbourhoods dimly and smokily lit by whale-oil lamps. There were concerts, dinners, gentlemen's clubs, gardens in which to stroll and dally. Throughout the year, there were special events like Bartholomew Fair and Southwark Fair with rope dancers, puppets and wild animals. In the winter of 1788, the Thames froze over and the capital hosted one of its rare and magical frost fairs with the river becoming a frozen highway of booths and spectacles. The nightlife of London was famous. David Garrick at Drury Lane Theatre had developed a style of acting and performance that favoured the naturalistic, bringing a new dramatic energy to plays and influencing other actors. From a young age, Mary loved the theatre. She saw Garrick perform once. 'I was too young to understand much about his acting,' she said; 'I only knew I thought it was mighty fine.' As adults, she and Charles went to plays frequently; they liked to sit down in the pit at Drury Lane Theatre, as close to the stage as possible. She made Emily Barton, one of Mrs Leicester's pupils, give a lively account of a visit to the theatre to see *The Mourning Bride*:

... After the curtain drew up, I looked up towards the galleries, and down into the pit, and into all the boxes, and then I knew what a pretty sight it was to see a number of happy faces ... the common people were coming bustling down the benches in the galleries, as if they were afraid they should lose their places ... how leisurely they all came into the pit, and looked about them, before they took their seats ... It was a pretty sight to see the remainder of the candles lighted; and so it was to see the musicians come up from under the stage. I admired the music very much.

Mary could write well about the countryside and she shared the Romantic sensibility of the age, being stimulated and uplifted by nature, but there was also something in her that responded to the crude vigour offered by a city. Flowers and fruit bushes and shepherds were all very well but a noisy, bustling city street was the best sight in the world. And, in the story of Emily Barton, there is a little girl responding with her whole heart and soul to the thrills of theatre, appreciating the wonder and magic and possibility of art. It was a response that Mary understood and shared.

Chapter 2

A Little Learning

It proved to be a very large library. This was indeed
a precious discovery. I looked round on the books
with the greatest delight. I thought I would read
them every one.
    'The Young Mahometan', Mary Lamb, 1808

There's not a more productive source
Of waste of time to the young mind
Than dress.
    Poetry for Children, Charles and Mary Lamb, 1809

CLEVER, IMAGINATIVE AND SENSITIVE, Mary Lamb would
have been a pleasure to teach and London was full of
schools that would have suited her. Near her home, a Mrs
Briscoe ran an establishment offering tuition in French, Latin,
drawing and music. At another, a Mrs Makin taught history
and geography as well. Mrs Merribah Lorrington, the daughter
of an Anabaptist, offered what she called a 'masculine education' in French, Latin and Italian, arithmetic and astronomy,
until her fondness for drink brought the school into disre-
pute. Other schools specialised in teaching young ladies how
to dance, sing, play the piano, paint watercolours and all the

other activities described by Jane Austen characters as 'accomplishments'.

Instead, Mary was sent to Mr William Bird's Academy near the Temple, which, despite its rather impressive title, was essentially an undistinguished day school, similar to a dame school but for older children. It was the sort of establishment where, for about eight pennies a week, the children of shopkeepers and artisans were scrambled into a little learning, just enough to keep them in a similar line of work and the same social groove as their parents.

Bird himself was, according to Mary's brother Charles, who also attended the school, 'squat, corpulent, middle-sized, with something of the gentleman about him'. He wore a flowered Indian robe and was enthusiastic about corporal punishment, keeping a collection of beating equipment that included a whip and a ferule that raised blisters on the skin. But it was the assistant master, Benjamin Starkey, who made the biggest impression on Mary. At a young age, Starkey had been made a 'bound apprentice' to William Bird. He was deeply religious and clearly hated teaching. Once he ran away from the school and was brought back again, dejected and defeated, by his father. He was one of those mild, ineffectual, easily bullied creatures who, placed in front of a class, are swiftly and ruthlessly demolished by their pupils. Mary and the other girls tormented him but there was also something about him – his unhappiness perhaps or his evident unfitness for his position in life – that struck a sympathetic chord in her.

Decades later, in 1825, freed from the tyranny of Bird, but ill in hospital and depressed by the failure of his own school, Starkey wrote his memoirs in a magazine called the *Every Day Book*, prompting a reply from both Mary and Charles who were friends with the editor. 'If any of the girls who were my school-fellows,' wrote Mary, 'should be reading, through their aged spectacles, tidings from the dead of their youthful friend Starkey, they will feel a pang, as I do, at ever having teased his gentle spirit. They were big girls, it seems, too old to attend his instructions with the silence necessary; and however old age, and a long state of beggary, seem to have reduced his writing faculties to a state of imbecility, in those days, his language occasionally rose to the bold and figurative, for when he was in despair to stop their chattering, his ordinary phrase was, 'Ladies, if you will not hold your peace, not all the powers in heaven can make you.'

In William Bird's one schoolroom, Mary crammed herself into a small, sloping wooden desk, looking out, if she wanted, into a dull and dingy garden. She learned to read, write and do a little basic arithmetic. It was there she saw her first play, a production of *Cato* performed by the boys, a memorable experience but not one that made up for the inadequacy and paucity of her general education. Benevolent patrons at the Inner Temple served her brothers well, helping them to places at Christ's Hospital School. Venerable and prestigious, this school, which still exists, though no longer based in London, was founded in 1552 by King Edward VI as an establishment for the education of the poor. Many of its early pupils were literally taken off the streets. Its guiding aims had been to take children, some as young as babies, and care for and instruct them so that: '. . . neither in his infancy shall want virtuous education and bringing up, neither when the same shall grow into full age shall lack matter whereon the same may virtuously occupy himself in good occupation or science profitable to the commonweal'. Its records of 1582 show that it took in: 'every sortes of the poore . . . 200 ydell vagabondes . . . 300 fatherless children . . . 350 poore men overburdened with their children . . . 400 aged persons . . . 650 decayed householders . . . 200 sore and sicke persons'.

By the middle of the eighteenth century, a place at the school had become highly coveted. Increasingly, it became not so much a safety net for the destitute as a place where the canny and relatively well connected wangled themselves a free, classical education for their sons, although it retained enough of its earlier charitable values to have a distinctively varied intake. One of its old boys, Leigh Hunt, a life-long friend of the Lambs, remembered two boys at the school: 'one of whom went up into the drawing room to his father, the master of the house; and the other, down into the kitchen to his father, the coachman'.

Christ's Hospital divided its pupils into three clearly demarcated schools and prepared them efficiently for their different roles in life. The writing school made boys ready for commercial apprenticeships, the mathematics and drawing schools turned out future Navy men, while the Grammar School concentrated on educating boys for the law, Army or the Church. The most gifted of the Grammar School boys were known as Deputy Grecians, and three or four every year were full Grecians and destined for Oxford. Christ's Hospital boys wore distinctive uniforms – a blue-skirted gown, yellow stockings and tiny black worsted cap. A leather girdle completed the quaint ensemble that had apparently been the dress of ordinary Tudor schoolboys.

John and Charles were lucky: their school broadened their horizons, brought them new friends and interests. At Christ's Hospital, Charles laid the foundations of enduring attachments with the future poet Samuel Taylor Coleridge and the future political writer, Leigh Hunt. Mary spent too short a time at Mr Bird's Academy – perhaps as little as six months – to make a lasting female friend.

She fared better outside school. Her father's employer, the easy-going Samuel Salt, allowed the Lamb children free access to his library. The will Salt made in 1786 showed him to have owned works by Pope, Swift, Shakespeare, Addison and Steele. Standard inclusions in the library of an eighteenth-century gentleman were Bunyan's *The Pilgrim's Progress*, Foxe's *Book of Martyrs*, *The Whole Duty of Man*, Baker's *Chronicles*, *The Complete Letter Writer*, *Robinson Crusoe*, *Robin Hood's Garland*, *The Seven Champions*, Turner's *Spectator*, Culpeper's *Herbal* and Swift's *Tale of a Tub*. By modern standards, it would have been a relatively meagre collection but, to a young girl, hungry to learn and starved of resources, it must have been a feast. It was an eclectic mixture of poetry, plays, essays and religious writings of the intensely Protestant kind. Like many a clever, lonely child, Mary loved reading. In one of her short stories, 'The Young Mahometan', she recalled the joy of bookshelf browsing, the satisfaction of unchecked access to books. The heroine, Margaret Green, is let loose inside the library of a great country house, finding it 'a precious discovery'. 'If you never spent whole mornings alone in a large library, you cannot conceive the pleasure of taking down books in the constant hope of finding an entertaining book among them,' says Margaret. Ignored by her mother, who 'had almost wholly discontinued talking' to her, Margaret's mind enters easily into the fictional world of *Mahometism Explained* and she becomes convinced that she is a Mahometan and that her mother who has not read the book isn't and is therefore in danger of destruction. Anxiety about her mother makes her feverish and a doctor is called to her rescue. He prescribes a jolly outing to a fair and the company of other girls and, in the real world, surrounded by friendly faces and listening to lively voices, Margaret recovers her spirits. It was a fascinating exploration by Mary of the powerful effect literature can have on an imaginative child. It was also eloquent in its evocation of the loneliness felt by a neglected one. 'I scarcely ever heard a word addressed to me from morning to night,' says Margaret.

Although the holidays at Christ's Hospital School were generous – forty days a year – Mary was separated from her beloved brother. However much she read by herself, there was no disguising the gap between her brothers' education and her own, a divide that was most clearly demonstrated by the acquisition of Latin. To be able to read the Classics was the mark of the gentleman, the evidence of a quality education. The Lambs' collection *Poetry for Children* contained a poem called 'The Sister's Expostulation on the Brother's Learning Latin'.

Shut these odious books up, brother –
They have made you quite another
Thing from what you us'd to be –
Once you lik'd to play with me –
Now you leave me all alone,
And are so conceited grown
With your Latin, you'll scarce look
Upon any English book.
We had us'd on winter eves
To con over Shakespeare's leaves,
Or on Milton's harder sense
Exercise our diligence –
And you would explain with ease
The obscurer passages,
Find me out the prettiest places,
The poetic turns, and graces,
Which alas! Now you are gone,
I must puzzle out alone,
And oft miss the meaning quite,
Wanting you to set me right,
All this comes since you've been under
Your new master. I much wonder
What great charm it is you see

In those words, musa, musae:
Or in what they do excel
Our word, song. It sounds as well
To my fancy as the other.
Now believe me, dearest brother,
I would give my finest rock,
And my cabinet, and stock
Of new playthings, every toy,
I would give them all with joy.
Could I you returning see
Back to English and to me.

The feelings of exclusion and loss are very strong. And 'The Brother's Reply', the poem's companion piece, recognises that sense of rejection and ends with understanding and reassurance.

But if all this anger grow
From this cause, that you suspect
By proceedings indirect,
I would keep (as misers pelf)
All this learning to myself;
Sister, to remove this,
Rather than we will fall out,
(If our parents will agree)
You shall Latin learn with me.

By dint of her own determination and with Charles's help, Mary did manage to learn Latin but not until she was in her forties, when she mastered it well enough to teach it to children and to make a pun in that language. 'Sic transit gloria Munden,' she said when watching the farewell performance of the comedian Joseph Munden. She said she bothered to learn Latin only because she was worried about her 'inability to write' and that she worked at it 'merely to assist her in acquiring a correct style'. But she was underplaying her keenness; acquiring Latin helped her overcome the feeling of inadequacy gained in her childhood.

Self-taught, she was also self-doubting. She was particularly sensitive about her handwriting. 'I have so often felt the disadvantage of my own wretched handwriting,' she once lamented. And she added to one letter, the embarrassed postscript, 'Did you ever see such a queer scrawl as mine?' As an adult, she preferred to use lined paper and she wrote a sonnet, 'Written in the First Leaf of a Child's Memorandum Book', on the difficulties of writing neatly:

> My neat and pretty book, when I thy small lines see,
> They seem for any use to be unfit for me.
> My writing, all misshaped, uneven as my mind,
> Within this narrow space can hardly be confin'd.
> Yet I will strive to make my hand less awkward look;
> I would not willingly disgrace thee, my neat book!
> The finest pens I'll use, and wond'rous pains I'll take,
> And I these perfect lines my monitors will make.
> And every day I will set down in order due,
> How that day wasted is; and should there be a few
> At the year's end that shew more goodly to the sight,
> If haply here I find some days not wasted quite,
> If a small portion of them I have pass'd aright,
> Then shall I think the year not wholly was misspent,
> And that my Diary has been by some good Angel sent.

Charles said that Mary wrote 'a pretty good style' and 'had some notion of the force of words' but he too agreed that her handwriting was 'poor'. He wrote a characteristically exaggerated and teasing description of her 'pimping, mean, detestable hand'. 'She is ashamed of the formation of her letters,' he joked. 'There is an essential poverty and abject-ness in the frame of them. They look like begging letters. And then she is sure to omit a most substantial word in the second draft (for she never ventures an epistle, without a foul copy first) which is obliged to be interlined, which spoils the neatest epistle. Her figures 1,2,3,4&c . . . are not figures but Figurantes. And the combined posse go staggering up and down shameless as drunkards in the day time.' Actually, her handwriting was perfectly fine – the elegant, right-slanting eighteenth-century copperplate with its long downstrokes and thin, light upstrokes – but it took her a long time to get over her sense of inferiority. And some things she never learned. Her spelling remained erratic throughout her life – she sometimes spelled holiday with two ls and she relied on Charles to correct her grammar.

Her brothers, with their classical education and good hand-writing skills, were expected to take up quasi-genteel positions as clerks. Mary, it was decided, was to be a seamstress. At some point in her teens – no record remains of the significant events in Mary's young life – she was apprenticed as a mantua maker and trained to make ladies' clothes. According to *A Description of All Trades*, a 1747 handbook, compiled so that: 'parents, guardians and trustees may, with greater ease and certainty, make choice of Trades agreeable to the capacity, education, inclination, strength and fortune of the youth under their care', the trade of a mantua maker was a good one. The anonymous career adviser wrote that, 'This trade belongs entirely to the women, both as to the work and the wear, and a very extensive one it is, as well in the country as in the City. It is reckoned a genteel as well as profitable employ, many of them living well and saving money. They take girls and young women apprentices (who must work early and late as business calls) with whom they have from 5 to 20 guineas, according to the degree of their business, which with some is very large. As to journeywomen they have generally 7 or 9s a week; and to make a mistress, there is little else wanting than a clever knack at cutting out and fitting, handsome carriage, and a good set of acquaintance.'

The air of gentility would have gratified Mary's parents and sewing skills were essential for any girl aspiring to be a lady's maid. They were probably preparing her for a life in service. So while Charles struggled with the conjugation of Latin verbs, Mary got to grips with the construction of the mantua. Typically, this outfit consisted of a bodice and a skirt underneath, the latter cut away to show the petticoat which was often of a contrasting material. The wearers probably thought it was delightfully pleasing and simple but the seamstress knew it was the very devil to make, involving the sort of deceptively simple draping and pleating that takes hours to get right. It used yards of easily spoilt material like silk, damask and muslin, and fashions changed with such bewildering speed, it was a full-time job to keep abreast of them. Mary's interest in clothes only ever became professional, never personal. Her training gave her the ability to appreciate well-made clothes and she had a good sense of fabric, but it was the skill in the work and the quality of the raw materials she was admiring, not the fashion. She once declared herself to be 'mainly ignorant' about the 'newest and most approved modes' and Charles talked of her 'paddling about for a cheap gown'. Her own preference was for clothes that were practical and neat. One observer described her as 'dressed with Quaker-like simplicity in dove-coloured silk, with a transparent kerchief of snow-white muslin folded across her bosom'. Another said, 'her apparel was always of the plainest kind; a black stuff or silk gown, made and worn in the simplest fashion'. For an intelligent girl who loved books and envied her brother his Latin studies, women's fashion was an unsuitable and frustrating business to be in. Customers were notoriously difficult to please. R. Campbell, the author of the 1747 *London Tradesman*, described the difficulties faced by mantua makers. 'She must learn to flatter all Complexions, praise all shapes, and in a word, ought to be complete mistress of the art of dissimulation. It requires a vast stock of patience to bear the tempers of most of the customers, and no small share of ingenuity to execute their innumerable whims.'

However skilled Mary became at 'cutting out and fitting', living as she did in the Inner Temple she lacked genteel female acquaintances and, as to carriage, she was short and had a slight speech impediment. Moreover the assertion in *A Description of All Trades* that the mantua-making business was 'profitable' was inaccurate. In fact, all sewing work was notorious for its low pay, long hours and a tendency to drive its practitioners to physical and moral ruin. It ruined a woman's eyesight and sapped her strength. Campbell said that the business had 'small reputation'; it was so badly paid that it was commonly believed that the only way for a seamstress to survive was to supplement her earnings by prostitution. If she lacked friends, he said, 'it is more than ten to one but she takes some idle, if not vicious course'.

Mary's meagre salary might have been bearable if it had continued to be merely an addition to the family finances. But a series of blows knocked the Lamb family badly off course. In 1792, her grandmother Mary Field and her father's employer Samuel Salt both died. The death of the first was a private sorrow but the loss of Salt was a disaster. In the four years that followed, the Lambs sailed towards the brink, then beyond, of disaster.

The Lambs had been wholly dependent on Salt. He had given them a home as well as an income. Thanks to him, Mary had enjoyed access to books she wouldn't otherwise have seen and her brothers had been educated well above the family's means. That the family lived somewhere as beautiful and grand as the Inner Temple was due to the fact that Salt employed John Lamb. Thanks to him and – and also to their grandmother, Mrs Field – they had seen how the rich lived, but they were not rich themselves. They lived among the gentry, knew how it fed and clothed itself but they didn't belong there. Their stake in the world represented by Blakesware and the Inner Temple – a world of affluence and privilege – was only leasehold.

Salt remembered his servants in his will: 'to my servant John Lamb, who has lived with me near forty years £500 South Sea stock. To Mrs Lamb £100 in money well deserved for her care and attention during my illness.' A codicil asked his executors to employ John Lamb to receive his 'Exchequer Annuities of £210 and £14 during their term' and to pay him £10 a year for his trouble. The codicil left a further £100 to Mrs Lamb. The stock would have brought in about £20 a year and the money was, of course, welcome but not as useful as the chambers and the annual salary of just over £32 a year. And John Lamb's health was gone; he'd suffered what, judging from its symptoms, was probably a stroke. In January 1793, he asked the Inner Temple authorities to relieved him of some of his duties. He was no longer able to wait at table as 'he had nearly lost the use of his left hand, and was otherwise very infirm'. He and his family had to leave the Temple. So along with her sick father, her elderly mother and aunt and young brother, Mary passed through the Pegasus Gates for the last time. Their new home was just a few blocks north-west of the Inner Temple in Little Queen Street but it was so run-down and squalid it could have been another world.

Charles and her elder brother John were working as clerks

The house on Little Queen Street.

– the former at the East India House and the latter at South Sea House; they were both accounting drones in these massive commercial and colonial enterprises. John lived away from home and Charles was making the most of his leisure time, enjoying, in a low-cost way, being a young man about town. He and a collection of friends from school took to meeting at the Salutation and Cat, an inn opposite Christ's Hospital where they gathered to drink egg nog and smoke tobacco. These evenings out must have seemed like the most glittering of balls to his Cinderella sister. Her mind was taken up with ailing parents, domestic chores and sewing work, while theirs, like countless young men before and after them, were preoccupied with the great things they would do, the books they would write, the radical politics they would put into action, the women they would love. They were an exciting bunch. There was Robert Southey who was supposed to be going into the Church but who called himself an atheist. He had written a poem about Joan of Arc, pages and pages of it, all bound up with green silk ribbon. There was Jem White, another Bluecoat who, in collaboration with Charles, was enjoying himself writing the 'original' letters of Shakespeare's Sir John Falstaff. There was Valentine le Grice who liked practical jokes and who enticed Charles away from the Salutation and Cat to drink Burton ale with him at the Feathers Inn in Holborn.

Chief, though, among these cronies was Samuel Taylor Coleridge. Although this was not yet the famous Coleridge, the writer of *The Ancient Mariner* and *Kubla Khan*, he was still something special. After Christ's Hospital, he had gone to Cambridge, then given up his studies to enlist as a soldier; the Army had quickly realised how unsuitable he was and kicked him out. Now he was in London, restless, excitable and inspiring. He was engaged to one woman (his future wife Sarah) and infatuated with another, Mary Evans. He was, also, head over heels in love with the philosophy of Pantisocracy, and busy putting the finishing touches to a plan to go with a group of friends to Susquehanna in America and start up an ideal colony.

Mary knew Coleridge and was as fascinated by him as Charles was. And although she couldn't join them in their writing and their drinking, she appeared in their poetry. Coleridge, who had been deeply affected by the love and care of his dead sister Nancy, was fascinated by the relationship between Mary and Charles. He was fond of her and he was even fonder of her fondness for Charles. The two men's love and admiration for Mary, though deep and sincere, was also a way of expressing their strong feelings for each other; she was not a muse so much as a shared reference point, a place where their minds and feelings met. In December 1794, Mary was sick and Coleridge was moved to describe the relationship between brother and sister. 'His sister has lately been very unwell – confined to her Bed dangerously – She is all his Comfort – he her's. They dote on each other.' Her illness also became the subject of a poem that he sent to Charles.

> In fancy (well I know)
> From business wandering far and local cares,
> Thou creepest round a dear-loved Sister's bed
> With noiseless step, and watchest the faint look,

Soothing each pang with fond solicitude,
And tenderest tones medicinal of love . . .
          Cheerily, dear Charles!
Though thy best friend shall cherish many a year:
Such warm presagings feel I of high Hope.
For not uninterested the dear Maid
I've viewed – her soul affectionate yet wise,
Her polish'd wit as mild as lambent glories
That play around a sainted infant's head.

As if in answer, when Charles fell ill at the end of 1795, he
wrote a poem addressed to Mary and sent it to Coleridge.

          To My Sister
If from my lips some angry accents fell
Peevish complaint, or harsh reproof unkind,
'Twas but the error of a sickly mind,
And troubled thoughts, clouding the purer well,
And waters clear of Reason; and for me
Let this my verse the poor atonement be –
My verse which thou to praise were e'er inclined
Too highly, and with a partial eye to see
No blemish: thou to me didst ever shew
Fondest affection, and would'st oft times lend
An ear to the desponding love-sick lay.

Charles's malady was more serious than Mary's; he had suffered
a nervous breakdown. He blamed his collapse on his failed
courtship of a young Hertfordshire girl called Ann Simmons;
his brother John thought it was due to the pernicious influence of the wayward and mercurial Coleridge. Whatever the
reason, he was in an asylum for six weeks. He faced his illness
with bravado, calling it a 'temporary frenzy' and claiming to

have spent the time in the asylum 'very agreeably'. He wrote to Coleridge: 'Dream not, Coleridge, of having tasted all the grandeur and wildness of Fancy, till you have gone mad.' While incarcerated, Charles had been delirious, fancying himself as Young Norval, a hero of a Scottish play and ballad. Norval is a foundling, cast out of his aristocratic home, brought up by a shepherd. He then returns to save his father's life and be reunited with his mother. But Randolph's heir kills Norval and his grief-stricken mother hurls herself off a cliff. One wonders exactly what uncomfortable emotional currents were swirling around the Lamb household at that time. Mary had suffered too, fretting and anxious over his health. Mentally she was weakened, aware as always of 'a certain flightiness in her poor head', said Charles.

Things were going badly with the Lambs. A few months after Charles's breakdown, the elder brother John Lamb had an accident. Strong winds blew a stone down upon his leg and, for a while, it looked as if it might need to be amputated. Once again, Mary probably added nursing to her other duties. Her mother was ill too; a physical complaint, possibly arthritis, left her more and more dependent on Mary's care. Robert Southey visited them in Little Queen Street around this time and later recalled the family's misery. 'They were evidently in uncomfortable circumstances. The father and mother were both living; and I have some dim recollection of the latter's invalid appearance. The father's senses had failed him before that time.'

By the summer of 1796, according to Charles, his mother was 'entirely helpless (not having the use of her limbs)'. Mary was virtually a prisoner of her mother's illness as she was 'necessarily confined from ever sleeping out, she being her bed fellow'. Mary did not spare herself when it came to looking after her family. To her mother, 'every act of duty and of love

she could pay, every kindness...through a long course of infirmities and sickness, she could shew her, she ever did,' said
Charles. Mary was 'thoroughly devoid of the least tincture of
selfishness'.

She was still working diligently at her sewing but, however
hard she worked, even if she cut and stitched for eighteen
hours a day, it was impossible for her to support her family.
There were, quite simply, too many seamstresses in London
and, unless you were the owner of a large establishment, you
could not afford to buy material in enough quantities to get
discounts. And just to make the odds of success even lower,
there was a widely held view that a good wife and mother
should make a substantial portion of her family's clothes rather
than employ someone else to do it. The result was that, aside
from the few fashionable seamstresses who kept fashion spies
in Paris and served the aristocracy, most mantua makers barely
earned enough to keep themselves alive. Mary became one of
what the social reformer, John Pickmere, called the 'thousands
of young females' who were 'necessitated by the pecuniary
misfortune of their parents to earn a livelihood by needlework'. Many of them 'having in vain sought for a slender
pittancy, their parents being either dead or through misfortunes unable to provide for them ... in a moment of despair,
resort to prostitution and its concomitants, misery, disease and
death'.

There was no prostitution in Mary's life but everything else
that Pickmere described was there – misery as she sewed for
everyone's dear life, disease as her parents deteriorated before
her eyes and, soon to come, violently and by her own hand,
death.

19th. William Clark, the driver of the Newmarket mail, was indicted for wilful murder. It appeared that the prisoner was driving the mail coach at a very furious rate along Bishopsgate-street, where he ran over a boy and killed him on the spot. The prisoner drove on not knowing of the accident, but was soon afterwards stopped. He alledged in his defence, that his employers were under contract to perform the journey within a certain period, and therefore he thought it his duty to drive so fast. The judge, in summing up the evidence, observed, " no contract could justify a man for driving in such a manner as to endanger the lives of others." The jury retired, and were absent two hours; when they returned, and found the prisoner, not guilty.

23d. This afternoon the coroner's jury sat on the body of a lady in the neighbourhood of Holborn, who died in consequence of a wound from her daughter, the preceding day. While the family were preparing for dinner, the young lady, in a fit of insanity, seized a case knife lying on the table, and in a menacing manner pursued a little girl, her apprentice, round the room. On the eager calls of her helpless infirm mother, to forbear, she renounced her first object, and, with loud shrieks, approached her parent. The child, by her cries, quickly brought up the landlord of the house, but too late; the dreadful scene presented to him the mother lifeless on a chair, pierced to the heart; her daughter yet wildly standing over her with the fatal knife; and the venerable old man, her father, weeping by

her side, himself bleeding at the forehead, from the effects of a blow he received from one of the forks she had been madly hurling about the room. For a few days prior to this, the family had discovered some symptoms of lunacy in her, which had so much increased on the Wednesday evening, that her brother, early the next morning, went in quest of Dr. Pitcairn; had that gentleman been providentially met with the fatal catastrophe had, probably, been prevented. She had once before, in the earlier part of her life, been deranged, from the harrassing fatigues of too much business. As her carriage towards her mother had been ever affectionate in the extreme, it is believed, that to her increased attentiveness to her, as her infirmities called for it, is to be ascribed the loss of her reason at this time. The jury without hesitation, brought in their verdict,—Lunacy.

24th. The melancholy account of the blowing up of the Amphion frigate, at Plymouth, was received at the Admiralty from Sir Richard King, by which it appears that Captain Pellew, the first lieutenant, and fifteen of the crew, out of 220, are the only survivors left to relate the dismal catastrophe; Captain Swaffield o the Dutch prize, is among the unfortunate victims. The accident happened at a quarter past four on Thursday afternoon, while the Captain and his friends were at dinner. Mr. Pellew is dangerously wounded. Every exertion that could be used was rendered by the ships boats in the harbour.

28th. This morning a convocation was held at St. Paul's Cathedral. This is a ceremony which

The *Morning Chronicle*'s report of the murder.

Chapter 3

A Day of Horrors

The fact itself is too notorious to be denied; the first
phenomenon by which despair, arising from a desire
of ease from pain through the medium of death,
exhibits itself, is often the murder of another.
Sir Alexander Chrichton, An Inquiry into the
Nature and Origin of Mental Derangement, 1798

SOME SORT OF DISASTER was probably inevitable. As the
summer of 1796 drew to an end, Mary was living on a
knife-edge. The long days spent hunched over fabric, cutting
and stitching, measuring, pushing herself to finish her task,
were unravelling her. She hunched over her sewing until her
back ached, worked her needle until her fingers became numb
and peered at fabric until her eyes were blurred with tired-
ness. The precision required in sewing hid the rush of over-
wrought energy and nervous excitement building in her mind.

The demands of her parents, both ill in their different ways,
were endless. She was physically drained and mentally wound
up. From morning to night, she worked and worried, her daily
life encompassing the worst of both worlds – she was lonely,
isolated in her burden of work and care – but never left alone
to recoup her spirits. All her resources – time, energy, money,

skills – were pressed into a struggle to keep the feeble Lamb family afloat. No part of her life was truly her own, there was no minute of her day that was not already claimed in the service of someone else. Even at night, there was no privacy; she shared the bed of an elderly invalid. Insomnia is now recognised as a warning signal in manic-depressive illness and it was impossible that Mary could sleep properly in these circumstances. With sleep deprivation, that peculiarly disorientating and distressing mental state, problems are magnified tenfold and rational thought flies out of the window. That year, September was as hot as June – 78 degrees Fahrenheit – and working with fabric in that heat would have been miserable and oppressive. And September was traditionally a bad month for dressmakers. So added to the normal family worries over money, there was a seasonal dip in income.

Not just Mary but the entire family was buckling under its various pressures, with the result that there was no time to take care of her. Besides, in the Lamb family, taking care of people was Mary's job. In the midst of such general debilitation, Mary's troubled behaviour – agitation, irrationality, excitement – must have seemed relatively minor and, it was to be hoped, short-lived. By the evening of Wednesday 21 September, it was clear to everyone that she was getting worse; her condition was serious. On Thursday morning, Charles left the house early and went to find Dr Pitcairn, the medical man who had treated him during his own breakdown. Pitcairn had an excellent reputation. According to a contemporary, he was 'one of the most beloved and popular physicians of his day. Tall, erect and handsome, his practice included patients from every rank of society; he spent much time with them, and often forgot his fee – No Medical man, indeed of his eminence in London, perhaps ever exercised his profession to such a degree gratuitously.' Since 1780 he had been Physician to St Bartholomew's

Hospital. He was a man who inspired confidence, perhaps he could have helped Mary, perhaps he could have saved her mother but Charles could not find him. Unsuccessful, he then went on to his office at the East India House.

Back in Little Queen Street, events moved quickly. Mary became increasingly excited, she was distracted and confused, her speech was incoherent. She was irritable when crossed or contradicted. As the day wore on, the tension mounted. Around three o'clock in the afternoon – the time when unfashionable people like the Lambs dined – she cracked. The scene was set for a family meal, not a tragedy. The cutlery, forks and a case-knife – a long, sharp-pointed carving knife made of iron with a forged steel edge, used for carving meat – was already out on the table. Then something – the sight of expensive fabric spoilt by carelessness perhaps or maybe a hint of defiance from her young apprentice, a sudden burst of extra loud noise from the street below, the sight of her hopeless, helpless family gathered together, waiting for their dinner – made Mary snap. She grabbed the case-knife, and went on the attack. It was violence born of despair, a strike against all the demons in her mind, against all the endless, wearing pressures in her life. Only there were real people in the room and she went for them too. Firstly, she chased her apprentice. The young girl screamed for help and then ran for her life. When her mother shouted to her to stop, Mary turned on her instead. An easy victim, Mrs Lamb could neither walk nor stand; she could not escape. The homely piece of cutlery became a fatal weapon. Mary stabbed her mother through the heart.

At that moment, Charles entered the room. He was not in time to save his mother but perhaps he prevented further attacks. 'I was at hand only time enough to snatch the knife out of her grasp,' he recalled. It was an act of bravery as Mary was raving; she had no idea what she was doing, never mind what she had just done. Charles got her out of the room, away from the blood and pain and fear and took her, still crazed and in broad daylight, through the crowded streets of London and had her admitted into Fisher House, a large lunatic asylum in nearby Islington. Given her crime, given her condition, staff at the asylum would almost certainly have placed her in a darkened room or under restraint, either by trapping her flailing arms in a straitjacket or by chaining her hands or feet to the wall or a bed. She was seen by a doctor and an apothecary and given drugs, 'an opening draught' which was either an emetic or something to open her bowels. There was, at the time, a common supposition that mad people were consti-pated. Alleviating that physical symptom would restore them to sanity. The root of white briony and syrup of violets were frequently used as purgatives.

While she raved behind the walls of the asylum, the law – the system that the Lamb family had served so faithfully – swung into action. A coroner jury sat on Mary's case and all the details of her violent crime and her sad life came out and were duly reported in the papers. *The Times* described her chasing the young apprentice 'in a menacing manner', and gave its readers harrowing details of her 'loud shrieks' as she advanced on her mother. It had her standing 'wildly' over her mother, 'madly hurling' forks about the room. In the news-paper's reports, she was like a model for madness, like one of Hogarth's Bedlam madwomen made flesh. Another newspaper, the *Morning Chronicle*, added more sympathetically that 'it seems the young Lady had been once before, in her earlier years, deranged, from the harassing fatigues of too much busi-ness. – As her carriage towards her mother was ever affec-tionate in the extreme, it is believed that to the increased attentiveness, which her parents' infirmities called for by day and night, is to be attributed the present insanity of this ill-fated young woman.' The *Evening Post* destroyed her anonymity by printing her name and profession. 'Miss Lamb, a mantua maker in Little Queen St, Lincoln's-Inn-Fields' was now a public figure. All the papers reported the jury's verdict: 'Lunacy.'

For ten days, Mary was out of her mind, lost to reason and to knowledge of her crime. Once the demon of madness left her, he took with him that merciful amnesia. She was forced to confront the enormity of what she had done and it was a terrible moment. Charles, who was the only member of her family to see her during this time, said she had to deal with a 'a dreadful sense and recollection of what has past, awful to her mind and impressive'. By killing her mother, Mary transgressed every law of man and nature. She killed the woman who gave her life, she robbed her brothers of a parent, she widowed her father. The sanctity of the mother is paramount; that is why the *Oresteia* is the most highly charged and powerful of the Greek tragedies. Her Christian faith and a certain robust clear-sightedness saved her from the extremes of guilt. She was lucky in that those close to her did not blame her for the death. To Charles, she was the 'unhappy and unconscious instrument of the Almighty's judgements' and he wrote admiringly of her 'religious resignation' and the 'sound judgement which, in this early stage, knows how to distinguish between a deed committed in a transient fit of frenzy, and the terrible guilt of a mother's murder'. She was, he said, 'calm and serene' but with 'a most affectionate and tender concern for what has happened'.

A month later, she seemed to have done more than just forgive herself; she had persuaded herself that her mother had forgiven her. 'I have no bad terrifying dreams,' she wrote to Charles. 'At midnight when I happen to awake, the nurse sleeping by the side of me, with the noise of the poor mad people around me, I have no fear. The spirit of my mother seems to descend, and smile upon me, and bid me live to enjoy the life and reason which the Almighty has given me – I shall see her again in heaven; she will then understand me better.'

Whether it was a dream or a delusion produced by a mind not yet returned to its normal state, this belief in her mother's forgiveness was a powerful and healing one for her. Later she was to talk of that time to her brother's friend Charles Lloyd, describing herself, 'on her recovery from the fatal attack, as having experienced, while it was subsiding, such a conviction, that she was absolved in heaven from all taint of the deed in which she had been the agent – such an assurance that it was a dispensation of Providence for good, though so terrible – such a sense, that her mother knew her entire innocence, and shed down blessings upon her, as though she had seen the reconcilement in solemn vision – that she was not sorely afflicted by the recollection.' She never forgot her mother – her 'dear mother' she once told a friend, was always in her 'poor head and heart'.

There was horror at Mary's crime but there was also kindness. Jess Annandale, the woman who ran the asylum, treated her indulgently, even affectionately. Charles said she was like 'one of the family, rather than of the patients'. But how was she to live? A coroner's jury had declared her a lunatic and she was frightened about her future. In particular, she was terrified of being sent to Bethlem, that grim public hospital for the insane, which since its foundation in 1247, had acted as a symbol of insanity, cruelty and despair. It actually took only a little over one hundred patients but its symbolic value as a degrading place where the mentally ill were alternately neglected and abused, their sufferings callously displayed for the amusement of visitors (the practice of daytripping to Bethlem was actually over by 1770), was huge. For Mary, as for many Londoners, it was part of the city's landscape of misery. She told keepers at the asylum that she would have to go to Bethlem, that her brother John would insist on it, that she had often thought, as she passed the building, that 'here it may be my fate to end my days'. That Fate had something far better in store for Mary was due to her own strength of character and her brother's devoted love.

Chapter 4

The Sorest Malady of All

*Mania tranquilla – thoughtfulness, profound taci-
turnity, a fondness for solitude, refusing all kinds of
sustenance. They will lament, weep and sigh heavily.
Mania furibunda – restless, or loquacious, haughty
and supercilious in their demeanour – suspicious,
fickle, irritable, particularly at meals – they entertain
an inveterate aversion to a particular person.*
William Pargeter, Observations on
Maniacal Disorder, 1792

AFTER THE KILLING, THE Lamb family tottered and fell.
Mary was in an asylum, her mother was buried at St
Andrew's Church in nearby Holborn and what was left of the
family had to find their way through the disaster. Mary's
brother John, still recovering from his leg injury, was totally
unable to cope. He was, according to Charles, 'kind and
brotherly' but he had 'taken his ease in the world and is not
fit himself to struggle with difficulties'. He was 'little disposed
... at any time to take care of old age and infirmities'. He
didn't think Charles should sacrifice himself for Mary; he
didn't want to help look after the old man. But Charles also
feared for his brother's mind, so perhaps all three of the Lamb

siblings had some experience of madness. 'God bless us all and shield us from insanity, which is the sorest malady of all,' he prayed.

Aunt Hetty was sent away to live with a rich old lady, a relative of the Lambs. And Charles and his father decamped from Little Queen Street with all its terrible memories and moved to a small, square, corner house in Pentonville, close to Mary's asylum. They still didn't know what to do with Mary. She was well aware, none better, that the family had barely enough money to stay afloat so where were the resources to care for her and keep her out of a pauper asylum? She was overwhelmed by a sense of worthlessness and asked for nothing for herself. She bore her situation, Charles said, 'as one who has no right to complain'.

There was no framework in law for dealing with a crime like Mary's. The insane, like beggars, were the responsibility of the parish, a duty they exercised under the Elizabethan Poor Act of 1601. In her case, the parish authorities suggested that Mary should be locked up indefinitely, others close to Charles advised the same, but he was adamant that she would not remain a prisoner – 'What she hath done to deserve, or the necessity of such an hardship, I see not,' he told Coleridge. No paperwork remains to show how Charles pleaded or who decided but he promised the authorities and he promised himself that he would take care of Mary and he was convincing. Mary's crime had forced him to grow up, turning him from a carefree boy into a thoughtful head of the family. He worked out their finances carefully. He estimated they would need 50 guineas – 60 at most – a year for Mary's care. 'If my father, an old servant maid, and I can't live and live comfortably on £130 or £120 a year we ought to burn by slow fires, and I almost would, that Mary might not go into an hospital.'

Charles Lamb by William Hazlitt.

There was soon an added pressure on the family's meagre finances; Aunt Hetty was sent home in December, the rich relative found her 'indolent and mulish'. She was a broken woman; according to Charles she 'never completely recovered' from 'the shock she received on that our evil day'. In February 1797, she died. The father, John Lamb, was physically frail and witnessing his wife's death had robbed him of the last vestiges of his reason. He was a demanding patient, insisting that Charles play cribbage with him night after night or ordering him to read aloud from his epic poem 'The Wedding Sparrow'.

Charles, while outwardly the strongest member of the family, was deeply miserable. He was lonely – Coleridge had left London – and his moods veered from a Christian acceptance of his terrible lot in life to total despair. He developed a crush on a young Quaker girl who lived nearby and, with it, a lifelong soft spot for Quakers and the Quaker religion. The calm, the white robes, their air of intense cleanliness soothed and charmed him. Hester Savory was nineteen, two years younger than Charles, and lived in Pentonville with her brother and two sisters. Charles never actually spoke to her, only saw her in the street, but he talked of himself as 'being in love with her' and the hopelessness of his passion only added to his misery. The one bright spot that year was a visit he paid to Coleridge that July where he was introduced to the poet William Wordsworth.

Mary, on the other hand, was experiencing her first taste of leisure for many years. She was away from home but then home had not been a pleasant place for her. In April 1797, she moved into private rooms in the countryside, in the then rural district of Hackney. It was only six months since the tragedy but she believed the worst of her illness was behind her. Charles wrote confidently to Coleridge: 'In one little half year's illness, and in such an illness of such a nature and of such consequences! To get her out into the world again, with a prospect of her never being so ill again – this is to be ranked not among the common blessings of Providence.' She took up her sewing but this time it was for pin money only, never again would she be responsible for the family finances. She had time to read books and she read avidly, quickly exhausting Charles's collection. It was the passion of a bookish girl, long deprived of literature, now able to relax and enjoy herself. As spring turned to summer and she regained her physical strength and the pendulum of her mind swung back to its resting place, she had time to realise how lucky she was. She had told Charles that she had her mother's permission to enjoy her life. It was a heady injunction to a woman of thirty-two whose life had, until then, been mainly one of hard work and self-sacrifice. She had committed a hateful crime and been rewarded with love, she had broken the law and been given her freedom. The act of violence that had torn the mother from life had released the daughter into a new way of living. She didn't yet know that her future life as Charles's companion, housekeeper and collaborator would be extraordinarily vivid and creative, but it was already apparent that it would be a thousand times more fulfilling than the health-destroying labour of a seamstress, or the endless and thankless drudgery as the unmarried daughter of an impoverished household. She might have sensed her potential but she had yet to discover her talent. Perhaps she had an inkling of it as she sat, blissfully alone, sewing or reading the books Coleridge sent her through Charles or making plans with her brother on his Sunday afternoon visits. For the strange, disquieting truth about the killing is that, for Mary, it was the best thing that could have happened. With that case-knife, she had cut the ties that bound her.

For Charles though, 1797 was a year of unmitigated suffering. His mother's death, his sister's madness, his father's senility, his aunt's death – he wrote poetry on all these themes. He was filled with grief, anguish at the killing, remorse at not having treated his mother properly, distressed beyond measure by his father's decrepitude. The poem 'Written on the day of my Aunt's Funeral' encompassed all these painful feelings.

Farewell good aunt!
Go though, and occupy the same grave-bed
Where the dead mother lies.
Oh my dear mother, oh thou dear dead saint
Where's now that placid face, where oft hath sat
Mother's smile, to think her son should thrive
In this bad world, when she was dead and gone;
And where a tear hath sat (take shame, O Son!)
When that same child has proved himself unkind.
One parent yet is left – a wretched thing,
A sad survivor of his buried wife,
A palsy-smitten, childish, old, old man,
A semblance most forlorn of what he was.
A merry cheerful man.

Mary's visions of a loving, all-forgiving mother had struck a chord with him and, as the grim anniversary of the day of horrors came round, he borrowed some of her words and feelings. The result was the poem, 'Written a Twelvemonth after the Events'.

Thou, and I, dear friend
With filial recognition sweet, shall know
One day the face of our dear mother in heaven;
And her remember'd looks of love shall greet
With looks of answering love; her placid smiles
Meet with a smile as placid, and her hand
With drops of fondness wet, nor fear repulse.

There is a movement towards resolution in the poem; bowing to God's will, appreciating the few friends left, he is carried forward 'To the not unpeaceful evening of a day / Made black by morning storms.' The anniversary meant both painful memories but also a sense of finality and closure.

He poured forth his feelings into these poems but he also edited them. From one – 'The Old Familiar Faces' – he cut the following lines:

> I had a mother, but she died, and left me
> Died prematurely in a day of horrors –

Some things were too painful for publication. The rest of the verses were collected together and published in a slim volume entitled *Blank Verse* alongside verses by Coleridge and Charles Lloyd. It appeared the following year and Mary would have read there a record of the total desolation of Charles's spirits, the despair that her matricide had caused. But she would also have read the dedication.

> The few following poems
> Creatures of the fancy and feeling
> In life's more vacant hours,
> Produced, for the most part, by
> Love in idleness,
> Are,
> With all a brother's fondness,
> Inscribed to
> Mary Ann Lamb,
> The author's best friend and sister

He wanted the inscription to be a surprise for her. 'There is a monotony in the affections, which people living together or, as we do now, very frequently seeing each other, are apt to give in to: a sort of indifference in the expression of kindness for each other, which demands that we should sometimes call to our aid the trickery of surprise,' he wrote to Coleridge. It was Mary's second appearance in print, a loving counterpoint to the dreadful exposure of the newspaper stories. The message of the dedication was clear. It was not just his poetry that he was giving to Mary but also all his love, all his care.

In April 1799, their father died. For his children, there must have been relief mixed in with their mourning. It put an end to a painful period in his life and, for Mary, it signalled the real beginnings of her new life. Her brothers buried him at St James's Church in Clerkenwell, the same resting place as his sister Hetty, and Mary prepared to leave her lodgings in London and join Charles in Pentonville. On the surface, things went well. There were no longer any parents to take care of and they were free to meet and spend time with whomever they wanted. They took long walks together and made new friends. They met Thomas Manning, a mathematician and a Chinese scholar, and the philosopher and novelist, William Godwin. They both became close to William Wordsworth and his sister, Dorothy. Wordsworth and Lamb talked poetry together while Mary asked Dorothy about her nieces and nephews and carried out book-buying commissions for her. Coleridge came to stay for five weeks in the spring of 1800 and Charles, for weeks afterwards, had to contend with 'a tribe of authoresses' – lion hunters like Sarah Wesley, the niece of the Methodist, and the novelist Elizabeth Benger. Partly amused, partly irritated, Charles called the first a 'mopsey' and complained that he had arrived home just in time to prevent Mary and Elizabeth Benger 'from exchanging vows of eternal friendship'. Benger was particularly hard to shake off. She invited them both to a party, fed them tea and macaroons and then patronised them mercilessly, speaking to them in French and talking about books they hadn't read.

Charles found time to visit Blakesware and enjoyed a jaunt to Cambridge. Best of all, Mary was well – 'she keeps in fine health,' he told Manning in March 1800, and 'we are all well and cheerful' he wrote to Coleridge in April. Then, just a month later, their newly constructed home life, their hopes, the entire edifice of their lives fell down. Their servant, Hetty, died and Mary broke down; Charles said it was 'in consequence of fatigue and anxiety'. She was so ill she had to return to the asylum and Charles wasn't even allowed to see her. He was in despair.

The re-appearance of insanity, so soon after setting up home with Charles, was a dreadful omen, a reminder that their domestic happiness was fragile, their peace of mind always at risk. Whatever they had hoped in the past, they were now forced to accept that Mary's illness could – and probably would – recur again and again. For Charles, the prospect was too much to contemplate. 'I almost wish Mary were dead,' he wrote to Coleridge, always the first port of call for his outpourings of emotion. He was 'completely shipwreck'd'. It wasn't just her suffering that pained him. He also needed her desperately. It took this breakdown of Mary's for him to appreciate how much he was dependent on her. In her absence, he couldn't bear to sleep in the house; the loneliness was so terrible he gave up the home in Chapel Street and went to stay with friends. He wrote to another friend: 'I expect Mary will get better, before many weeks are gone – but at present I feel my daily and hourly prop has fallen from me . . . I totter and stagger with weakness, for nobody can supply her place to me.'

When she was in a state of mania, Mary was an electrifying sight. Her brother's first biographer Thomas Noon Talfourd wrote how: '... her ramblings often sparkled with brilliant description and shattered beauty. She would fancy herself in the days of Queen Anne or George the First, and describe the brocades, dames and courtly manners, as though she had been bred among them, in the best style of the old comedy. It was all broken and disjointed, so that the hearer could remember little of her discourse; but the fragments were like the jewelled speeches of Congreve, only shaken from their setting. There was sometimes even a vein of crazy logic running though them, associating things essentially most dissimilar, but connecting them by a verbal association in strange order. As a mere physical instance of deranged intellect, her condition was, I believe, extraordinary; it was as if the finest elements of mind had been shaken into fantastic combinations like those of a kaleidoscope.' Knowing what she had once done, such an episode was frightening as well as thrilling. She could be violent. Coleridge recalled how, on one occasion, Mary took hold of him 'with violent agitation'. He described her, shortly before one attack, smiling 'in an ominous way'. There were many occasions when she had to be put in a straitjacket. After the violent phase there came a period of intense depressions. She talked of 'her drooping heart' and 'her poor head' or her 'dull head'. Sometimes her head felt 'cloudy'. In these moods, she was pitiable – 'miserably depressed in the most wretched desponding way conceivable' is how Charles once described her.

In between these attacks, she appeared and was totally sane. 'There was no tinge of insanity discernible in her manner to the most observant eye; not even in those distressful periods when the premonitory symptoms had apprised her of its approach and she was making preparations for seclusion,' wrote Talfourd. He praised the 'habitual serenity of her demeanour' and declared that she was 'remarkable for the sweetness of her disposition, the clearness of her understanding, and the gentle wisdom of all her acts and words.' One young friend and admirer of the Lambs, Charles Cowden Clarke, said that: 'Her manner was easy, almost homely, so quiet, unaffected, and perfectly unpretending was it.' Her behaviour was 'modest', her talking 'sparing' and her carriage 'retired'. William Hazlitt said Mary was the only thoroughly reasonable woman he'd ever met.

Her illness contributed to her feelings of self-doubt; she felt unable to trust herself. 'I have lost all self confidence in my own actions,' she wrote after a particularly bad episode left her shaken. 'One cause of my low spirits is that I never feel satisfied with any thing I do – a perception of not being in a sane state perpetually haunts me.' She was ashamed of these feelings and tried to combat them by sheer willpower.

Dr Pitcairn, for all his kindness and generosity, would have been unable to help. The doctors at the asylum would have been equally ineffective. It was Mary's misfortune that she was mad a hundred years before the German psychiatrist Emil Kraepelin wrote his detailed and definitive observations of the illness he called manic-depressive illness and paranoia. Mary's contemporaries accepted the verdict of lunacy but eighteenth- and nineteenth-century mental health literature was still preoccupied with defining exactly what they meant by that term. Today, there is, broadly speaking, a medical consensus on what madness is – it is a disease of the brain. Though there have been and still are dissenters – for example R. D. Laing who thought madness was a problem of family dynamics and Thomas Szass who thinks it's no more than a value judgement – mainstream thinking is that madness is biological (caused by a brain malfunction) and genetic (therefore hereditary). For Mary's doctors, there was as yet no mainstream. They saw madness as an intriguing and ongoing riddle and they wrote books that were a fascinating mixture of the medical, the philosophical and the sociological.

Lacking the modern certainty about the physical nature of madness, Mary's medical contemporaries had instead an intense interest in its cultural meanings. The titles were open-ended and questioning. Thomas Arnold finished his *Observations on the Nature, Kinds, Causes, and Prevention of Insanity* a decade before Mary killed her mother and his detailed catalogue of mental illnesses reads more like a list of human failings than a medical reference book. There was scheming insanity ('self conceit is one of its striking features') and 'bashful insanity' (shyness being the giveaway symptom). The romantically minded might worry because there were cases in which 'every instance of that extravagance and absurdity, in which the passion of love is abundantly fruitful, may be considered as a degree of insanity'. Observations, not conclusions or deductions, were also the theme of William Pargeter's *Observations on Maniacal Disorder*, which was published in 1792. Between 1792 and 1798, John Ferriar wrote up his thoughts in *Medical Histories and Reflections*. These writers were interested in the phenomenon of madness, absorbed in the stories of their patients, fascinated by the structure of the brain but never at all sure they had the answer. William Pargeter began his *Observations on Maniacal Disorder* with the rather endearingly humble statement: 'The original or primary cause of madness is a mystery and utterly inexplicable to human reason.' Many of the books at the time began with a wide open question – what is madness? Debate in medical circles centred on whether insanity was a disease or a symptom.

They were busy, these Georgian doctors. Busy cutting up the brains of dead madmen, busy examining their patients' heads to see if there was any link between hair colour and madness, busy wondering why it was that Methodists often went mad, and busy trying to understand why some women lost their minds after being seduced and deserted. They declared overwork and excessive study to be dangerous to the mind and railed against the fashionable trend toward keeping late hours and excessive tea drinking. They speculated, with a doleful pride, about the high incidence of madness in England; one doctor christened a disposition to suicide as Melancholia Anglica, and Arnold claimed that mental instability was increasing in England because of its 'excess of wealth and luxury'. Earlier, in 1733, Dr George Cheyne had written *The English Malady* and argued that social improvements were linked to insanity. He wrote: 'We have more nervous diseases since the present Age has made efforts to go beyond former times, in all the Acts of ingenuity, invention, study, learning, and all the contemplative and sedentary professions.' Certainly there was an English disposition to *write* about madness. John Haslam, the apothecary to the infamous Bethlem Hospital, noted in his 1798 treatise, *Observations on Insanity* that 'it has been somewhere observed, that in our own country more books on insanity have been published than in any other.'

This preoccupation with the nation's relationship to madness was due, in part, to the fact that the head of state, George III, had fallen victim to an alarming and, above all, well publicised bout of insanity in 1788. Eight years before Mary Lamb went mad and killed her mother, the nation had been riveted by daily bulletins on the king's madness. Its progress and prognosis was of huge significance for the government and for the nation. His Majesty's mental condition meant that there was an intense, ongoing interest in the topic of insanity. Whereas religion had been the talking point and the burning issue of the previous century, madness was the dominant subject of the eighteenth. When the king recovered, there was a national sigh of relief. Medals were struck to celebrate his recovery; one commemorated his doctor, the Reverend Francis Willis. The owner of a Lincolnshire madhouse, Willis was then elevated to superdoctor status. His apparent 'success' in 'curing' the king had two direct consequences – it speeded up the development of what we now call psychiatry, making it a distinct and discrete discipline within medicine, and it led to the widespread building of asylums. In 1788, when George III first went mad, there were twenty-two madhouses in London. By his death in 1820, there were more than double that number.

When all the observations, all the list-making and symptom tabulation failed, as it inevitably did, the doctors left their laboratories and scalpels and lists of observed symptoms and fell back, quite comfortably, on the ancient Greek system of the four humours – black bile, yellow bile, phlegm and choler. Within that system, an excess of black bile causes depression and an excess of yellow brings on mania.

And yet, they were often remarkably meticulous and accurate in their observations, and frequently insightful. Dr Pitcairn, who had treated Charles and who may have treated Mary, left no published writings but his influence can be felt in the work of one of his pupils. Dr Alexander Chrichton dedicated his 1798 book, *An Inquiry into the Nature and Origin of Mental Derangement comprehending a concise system of the physiology and pathology of the human mind and a history of the passions and their effects*, to his old teacher. In the section of his book entitled 'On Grief and Melancholy' he showed a keen understanding of how the mind behaved under pressure. A 'very common termination of despair is in murder,' he wrote in a passage that reads like an interpretation of Mary's case. When a person's 'health of body and energy of mind are greatly weakened and disturbed', when they have to, in addition, 'contend with poverty, obscurity, disappointment and neglect', it is not surprising when they give way to what he calls the 'desire for death' and 'lose

all command of mind'. The usual result is suicide, but sometimes the 'act of cruelty' is transferred 'from their own persons
to those of others'.

Sympathy and understanding was the best the doctors had
to offer Mary. Aside from the age-old techniques of cold baths,
purging, cupping, blistering and bleeding, the only treatment
doctors could offer Mary was incarceration. It was their main
tool for managing madness.

Whitmore House.

Chapter 5

Miss Lamb is from Home

That honour'd mind become a fearful blank
Her senses lock'd up, and herself kept out
From human sight or converse, while so many
Of the foolish sort are left to roam at large
> Charles Lamb, 'Written on Christmas Day',
> 1797

People may inveigh against the Bastille in France,
and the inquisition in Portugal, but I would ask if
either of these be in reality so dangerous or dreadful
as a private madhouse in England under the direction
of a ruffian
> Sir Launcelot Greaves, *Tobias Smollet*, 1762

THREE MILES FROM MARY'S Pentonville home lay Hoxton, a still rural district just outside the City of London; it had become, over the years, a byword for insanity. Hoxton Street itself was like a thoroughfare of madness; at the southern end lay the asylum, Hoxton House, another, Holly House, was a few hundred yards further up the road and, at the very top, loomed enormous Whitmore House. Mary's life involved an unhappy procession up this road. At first, she was looked after in Hoxton House, which catered mainly for paupers, and, as Charles's earnings increased, she moved to the far more expensive Whitmore, which prided itself on taking care of aristocratic lunatics. Mary talked of her 'banishment' to these places but the euphemism used for her many absences by her friends and by her brother was: 'Miss Lamb is from home.' This phrase, delicate and discreet, concealed the ugly realities that Mary faced whenever she was admitted to one of Hoxton's madhouses. Euphemism was too thin a cloak to conceal their cruelty and barbarism from Mary. The madhouses with their bolts and bars, their guards, their obscene rituals, were part of her life. For her, 'from home' was another, equally real, place.

Madhouses had long been a public scandal. Daniel Defoe had fumed in *August Triumphant*, published in 1728, that madhouses were a way for husbands to lock up their wives while they got on with committing adultery. A pamphlet in 1740 had declared them to be 'a public grievance' and claimed that: 'Wives put their husbands in them that they may enjoy their Gallants, and live without the observation and interruption of their husbands; and husbands put their wives in them, that they may enjoy their whores, without disturbance from their wives; children put their parents in them, that they may enjoy their Estates before their time; Relations put their Kindred in them for wicked purposes, guardians to cheat their pupils.'

Like Bethlem, the private madhouses carried an imaginative charge that was out of proportion to their actual influence. Mary Wollstonecraft's 1798 novel, *Maria or the Wrongs of Woman*, featured a young woman falsely imprisoned in a madhouse who nonetheless manages to conduct a passionate love affair with a fellow (also sane) inmate. In 1816 another novel, *Love in a Madhouse*, eroticised the same terrain of false imprisonment and forbidden love with its heady plot about a young rich girl who is incarcerated in an asylum when she refuses to marry a man of her guardian's choosing. Her lover then pretends to go mad in order to be incarcerated with her and thereby help her to escape. In the popular imagination, as in these fictions, injustice, love, sexual abuse and cruelty were an integral part of the madhouse, forming a powerful nexus of fear and fascination in which the real truth was almost obscured. The plain fact was madhouses were, quite simply, a racket.

The madhouse system had grown from simple roots – people looking for somewhere to put their insane relatives, and doctors and clergymen taking them into their homes and charging a fee. Once they became large establishments, economies of scale kicked in and they became highly lucrative. Francis Willis, who was credited with curing George III, had turned his home into a madhouse and always maintained that 'an accustom'd House for wrongheads' was an excellent proposition for his sons to inherit. In 1809, Andrew Duncan wrote in his *Observations on the General Treatment of Lunatics* that, 'Few speculations can be more unpleasant than that of a private madhouse, and it is seldom if ever undertaken, unless with the hope of receiving large returns on the capital advanced.' Sir Andrew Halliday, another critic of the system, railed against madhouse proprietors 'who have realized immense fortunes as wholesale dealers and traffickers in this species of human misery'.

These madhouses touted for business much as private schools or nursing homes for the elderly or cosmetic surgery clinics do today. Their adverts appeared in newspapers and were circulated on handbills and leaflets. Medical directories and books about insanity sold page space to madhouse proprietors. Like ambulance-chasing lawyers, they offered no win, no fee deals. One Jason Mason announced that he undertook 'to cure Hypochondriacs, Mad and Distracted People, with great success. No Cure No Pay Boarding excepted.' Who determined whether a patient was cured – and according to what criteria – was never spelled out. Some madhouses were grand; at Brislington House in Somerset, patients were allowed to keep doves, pheasants and greyhounds. But the commonest practice was to buy up a big house, put well-paying lunatics in the smart rooms and house the poor ones in the stables and outhouses. Buildings were never specially constructed for the purpose of caring for the mentally ill. Bethlem Hospital, whose name was synonymous with madness, had started life as the priory of St Mary's of Bethlehem.

Although an Act of Parliament of 1774 had ordered that madhouses be inspected and penalties levied where they found an inmate kept there without a written order from a physician, surgeon or apothecary, it was a toothless act and had nothing to say about standards in the houses. Some madhouse owners were doctors but there was no legal requirement that anyone associated with the establishment needed to have any medical training. William Pargeter insisted that abuse didn't happen in madhouses owned by doctors or clergymen while the businessmen owners included 'men who have just pecuniary powers sufficient to obtain a licence, and set themselves up keepers of private madhouse, alluring the public in an advertisement, that the patients will be treated with the best medical skill and attention . . . while at the same time, they are totally devoid of all physical knowledge and experience and in other respects extremely ignorant, and perhaps illiterate'.

Not only were there grave concerns about cruel practices, there were also doubts as to madhouses' effectiveness. Andrew Harper, an ex-Army physician and author of *A Treatise on the Real Cause and Cure of Insanity*, wrote that asylums might 'answer the purpose of private interest and domestic conveniency, but at the same time it destroys all the obligations of humanity . . . confinement never fails to aggravate the disease.

A state of coercion is a state of torture from which the mind, under any circumstances, revolts.' In short, madhouses were bad, dangerous, and didn't work.

Thanks to a Parliamentary committee in 1815, we know a lot about the conditions of the madhouses that became Mary's 'from homes'. In the years that she was in and out of Hoxton House, the asylum was owned by Sir Jonathan Miles, who described himself as being 'personally engaged in the management of the house'. He was an alderman of the City of London, becoming sheriff in 1806, and a knight in 1807. He had plenty of money, spending £10,000 in an attempt to win the rotten borough of Tregony in Cornwall in 1806, and was often suspected of bribery to gain his end. John Haslam, the apothecary at Bethlem, seemed to have some sort of understanding with Miles which meant that, when Bethlem was full, he directed patients to Hoxton. Miles's house had run into trouble when it was revealed he had received into the house a sane woman whose husband wanted to get rid of her. The woman had been held in Hoxton House for eight years, sometimes in chains. In the end, it was her determined mother and a Justice of the Peace who freed her.

Hoxton House took in paying patients like Mary, who had a room and attendant to herself, but the bulk of its inmates were pauper lunatics supported by their parishes, at sums ranging between eight and ten shillings a week. From 1792, it had had an agreement with the Admiralty to house naval men who'd been judged mad. Miles was secretive about Hoxton's conditions. Edward Wakefield (whose own mother had been confined to a madhouse) told a Select Committee that when he tried to inspect Hoxton House, he was refused admittance.

'I applied at Sir Jonathan Miles's receiving houses at Hoxton for leave to look over them; Mr Watt, the person who had the care of the house (Sir Jonathan Miles not living there) stated, that it was in the hands of trustees, who had determined that no persons would be permitted to look over the buildings; I argued with him the injury that he might do himself from such a refusal, and his answer was, that an inspection of that house would be signing its death warrant.'

Other inspectors who did manage to make it past the doorkeeper testified to the abominable conditions inside. Dr James Veitch, a staff surgeon in the Navy, damned the accommodation as 'exceedingly bad'. The floors were 'soaked with urine', everywhere it was 'all chaos and confusion'. The bedrooms were 'close, crowded, unventilated'. He saw patients forced to share narrow beds, men chained to benches and a sick man lying in such a room that 'the smell and nature of the apartment was utterly unfit for a human being to reside in, in any shape'.

The Inspector of Naval Hospitals, John Weir, called Hoxton 'radically defective' and thought it should be abandoned entirely and a special hospital built for naval lunatics. There wasn't enough bedlinen – inmates were expected to make do with loose straw. They ate standing up because there were no tables and with their hands as no cutlery was provided. There were few staff – as little as one attendant to twenty patients – and no attempt at treatment for any kind of illness. The mentally ill and the physically sick were lumped together to live or die, get well or worse, whichever came first. Patients who couldn't control their bladders or their bowels were left to dirty the floor or their beds. Sir Jonathan's attempts to bribe John Weir – he sent him gifts of fish and game, which were returned – had obviously not worked.

Some people did put in a good word for Hoxton House. A Mr James Birch Sharpe gave it a favourable report. He thought it was clean and the food adequate. But then, he was only twenty-six and for the previous five years Miles had paid his salary. The Committee censured Miles but, beyond that, he was not penalised in any meaningful way. Hoxton House remained in business until the early part of the twentieth century.

Superficially at least, Whitmore House – Mary's other asylum – was an improvement. Formerly the home of a Lord Mayor of London, it was an impressive building, 'a magnificent red brick mansion, with a sloping roof' according to one of its neighbours, the theatre impresario John Hollingshead. He said that 'it stood back in a planted courtyard, walled in with heavy gates, with an old-fashioned bell-pull at least two yards long and gardens enclosing lodges, stables, orchards, tall and sombre trees, and every feature of a grand old country mansion'.

It was a cut above Hoxton House. Giving evidence to the 1815 Select Committee, Edward Wakefield spoke enthusiastically of the 'very large gardens' and 'the general comfort and cleanliness of the house'. He was particularly impressed by the 'many small distinct houses' that stood in the gardens and 'the great enjoyment which a patient who has the means of paying for it, receives from living in a small house, surrounded by a garden, without the noise or the annoyance of violent maniacs about him'. Patients 'when convalescent, are allowed to amuse themselves by keeping fowls or rabbit, or cultivating a small piece of garden ground'. He thought the treatment in Whitmore House was 'in general good'.

And yet, it was also the subject of two highly damning reports. One was by John Mitford, who was a patient at Whitmore House between May 1812 and March 1813, the same years that Mary was also an inmate there. Mitford was a former Navy seaman, turned poet and journalist. After his spell in Whitmore House, he wrote *Crimes and Horrors in the Interior of Warburton's Private Mad-House at Hoxton, commonly called Whitmore House*. It offered a harrowing tale of unchecked abuse, written in a colourful, emotionally charged style. 'If there is in the breasts of men one sacred spark of love, humanity or pity, it will be called forth for helpless beings, lashed and tortured by fellows deserving of a gibbet; and where, both by men and women, deeds are done that shun the face of day, and enormities practised that cry aloud to heaven for vengeance,' is how he began his account.

Mitford described inmates being flogged with ropes by keepers, whipped until they bled, their mouths stuffed with human faeces and young female patients publicly gang-raped by their attendants. He wrote of patients left alone for days, chained to beds, without food and water. Most of his terror and his venom was aimed at the owner of Whitmore House, Thomas Warburton. This villain, he wrote, was

originally a butcher's boy in the country, and fled to London before he had served the term of his apprenticeship, for having a bastard-child swore to him. He was first employed under the porter at the gate of Whitmore House, to beat coats, clean shoes, and carry messages, for which he was rewarded with his meat. Being expert at conveying liquor into the house for the keepers to dispose of amongst their patients (a practice still pursued), he obtained a footing as a servant, and in that situation, by a little help, and much industry, he learned to read and write. His strength of body (a necessary qualification for a demon in one of these hells) and his zeal, raised him to the dignity of a keeper, and he assumed the control of the lash under happy auspices. He is more than six feet high, broad shoulders, heavy built, with knock knees, and a visage on which is a proboscis three inches long, quite sufficient to frighten a person of weak mind and delicate nerves into a fit of insanity. In time he obtained the confidential office of first keeper...and by the treatment of the lunatics under his care, gained the good graces of his mistress, who, upon the death of her husband, married him, and he became ruler of the mansion of affliction. Tom possessed a good deal of cunning and insinuating manners, which worked him into the good graces of many not awake to his duplicity.

Warburton was an empire builder of madhouses. Mary was just one of the eight hundred patients that Warburton had in his charge, distributing them across three houses in total. He also ran a kind of agency, providing nurses to private houses. Mitford explained how easy it was to deceive the commissioners appointed to inspect the madhouses. They were

permitted to visit between the hours of 9am and 5pm and though they took every precaution to prevent previous notice of their visit being made known to the licencees, the latter had, by some means or other, always been forewarned, and in this connection it is well to remember that it was an age when bribery and corruption was rife. The visits of the Commissioners never lasted longer than about three hours, and the Fellows were probably wined and dined by the Superintendent before the round of inspection. The Commissioners never inspected and questioned every patient, never visited every part of the asylum, and never insisted upon going on their round unaccompanied by the superintendents and keepers. The visiting physicians (the Commissioners) were not to blame if they made good reports upon visitation, the patients were better and more kindly used. Tommy himself sometimes dines with them in order that he might say 'oh, the patients live so well I frequently dine at their table from choice.

The house was cleaned in preparation for a visit, and new clothes given to those patients who normally wore rags. 'In

Warburton's houses, to save trouble and expense, and to allow the attendants some free time at the week-end, patients were placed in cribs at three o'clock on a Saturday afternoon, secured with chains and left there until Monday morning,' according to Mitford.

Mitford was clearly a man with a private grievance and the balance of his mind was upset; he later died an alcoholic in a workhouse. But many of his allegations are confirmed by John William Rogers, a more sober and measured medical man, who had been visiting surgeon to all Warburton's madhouses. He claimed that Warburton had dismissed him for being too humane in his treatment of the lunatics. In 1816, he published a pamphlet entitled *A statement of the cruelties, abuses and frauds which are practised in mad-houses*. He wrote of patients bruised and bleeding from being kept in leg irons, gagged with towels over their faces, violent force-feedings, men and women stripped and mopped at the yard pump.

Mary, as a paying patient, with a concerned and loving relative who visited regularly, may well have escaped the worst of the treatment meted out to inmates in these two madhouses. She may even have been one of the lucky few allowed to convalesce by keeping chickens at Whitmore House or wandering through the gardens of Hoxton. But there was a limit to how protected and sheltered she could be. When she was violent – and that was often the form her madness took – she would have been tied up, no matter how much money her brother was paying. She understood, because she had felt, the terrible vulnerability of the insane and their need for gentle care. She was familiar with the work of ill-trained and unkind nurses. She once wrote that she knew of 'many poor souls' afflicted with depression and knew too of the 'mismanagement with which I have seen them treated'. Writing to a friend whose mother was in an asylum, her advice was to make sure that she was 'treated with *tenderness*'. She stressed the word, because that simple quality, of which there was a shortage in Hoxton and Whitmore House, was 'a thing of which people in her state are uncommonly susceptible, and which hardly any one is at all aware of'. A hired nurse never understood, 'even though in all other respects they are good kind of people'.

Being forced to confront such terrible suffering, to be aware of such cruelties, was one of the worst aspects of Mary's illness. But she was gifted with the most marvellous powers of recovery. Not only did she always return from the heights of mania and the depths of despair, she faced, time and time again, the horrors of the madhouse, endured her banishment and then returned, back 'from home' to her home with Charles.

Chapter 6

The Sweet Security of Streets

But the clouds, that overcast
Thy young morning, may not last.
Soon shall arrive the rescuing hour
'To T.L.H. A child' Charles Lamb, 1814

WHERE WERE THEY TO live? It was a question Charles was always asking himself. He worried about how much neighbours knew about Mary, what they thought of her, how they would behave towards her. To Coleridge, he fretted 'her case and all our story is so well known around us . . . we are in a manner marked.' The image of cursing appeared several times; her illness, he thought, made them 'a sort of marked people'. He was aware of how isolated Mary was. There were families where he knew she wouldn't be welcome and he felt guilty when he went to any of them. There was, he said, 'something of dishonesty' in any pleasure he took without her. Poor Mary 'never goes anywhere'.

While Mary was undergoing her second spell in an asylum, he found a new home for them. Their new place – three rooms and a shared servant in Southampton Buildings in Holborn – came courtesy of an old schoolfriend who knew about Mary and appreciated that she would probably relapse again and again. Best of all, Southampton Buildings was in the thick of London, teeming, heaving, full-of-people London. In crowds, they felt safe, less exposed; Charles wrote to Manning, 'we can be no where private except in the midst of London'.

All that summer, the talk everywhere was of madness. On 15 May, King George III, no stranger to madness himself, was watching a play at Drury Lane Theatre when James Hadfield, a deranged ex-soldier, fired a pistol at him. Hadfield was tried for high treason but Dr Alexander Chrichton, who appeared in his defence, stated that he was suffering from paranoia caused by a head injury. Largely as a result of Chrichton's testimony, Hadfield was found not guilty on grounds of insanity. In response to this incident, Parliament passed the Act for the safe custody of Insane Persons Charged with Offences. It ordered that '. . . if they shall find that such a Person was insane at the Time of committing such offence, the court . . . shall order such Person to be kept in strict Custody, in such Place and in such Manner as to the Court shall seem fit, until His Majesty's Pleasure shall be known'. It meant that you could be legally not guilty but still subject to what was effectively imprisonment. To the Lambs, who knew exactly what Mary was capable of, the law had devastating implications. If she broke the law again, she could be locked up for life and no promise of shelter from a loving brother would free her that second time.

But as well as this new fear, the Lambs were also experiencing a new excitement, an outburst of energy that, for Mary, expressed itself in writing. That August, she wrote a poem and showed it to her brother. She wrote it to tease him for his admiration of a long-loved portrait of a woman that hung in the hall at Blakesware. This verse – Mary's first known piece of creative writing – was called 'Helen Repentant Too Late' and both she and her brother were delighted with it.

1

High-born Helen!
Round your dwelling
These twenty years I've pac'd in vain;
Haughty Beauty,
Your Lover's duty
Has been to glory in his pain.

2

High-born Helen!
Proudly telling
Stories of your cold disdain,
I starve, I die: –
Now you comply,
And I no longer can complain.

3

These twenty years
I've liv'd on tears,
Dwelling for ever on a frown;
On sighs I've fed,
Your scorn my bread·
I perish now you kind are grown!

4

Can I, who loved
My Beloved
But for the 'scorn was in her eye,'
Can I be moved
For my Beloved,
When she returns me 'sigh for sigh'?

5

In stately pride,
By my bedside
High-born Helen's portrait hung
Deaf to my praise;
My mournful lays
Are nightly to the portrait sung.

6

To that I weep
Nor ever sleep
Complaining all night long to her!
Helen grown old,
No longer cold,
Said 'You to all men I prefer. –'

It was not a great poem but the fact that she wrote it at all was evidence of not just a burst of creativity but also of a new-found zest for life and a confidence in herself and her own powers. Charles sent the poem to Coleridge. 'How do you like this little Epigram?' he asked, 'It is not my writing, nor had I any finger in it – if you concur with me in thinking it very elegant and very original, I shall be tempted to name the author to you. I will just hint that it is almost or quite a first attempt.' By writing that poem, Mary was signalling her wish to join Charles and Coleridge, to enter into the intimate world created by the two men through their writing. She had been a passive player in the serious game of poetry that went on between Charles and Coleridge, serving as their subject matter. With Helen, in a small but significant way, she showed that she wanted to take part. She was finding her voice.

Helen might have been a tease but, a few years later, Mary returned to the theme of lofty beauty with 'Lines Suggested by a

Picture of Two Females by Leonardo Da Vinci'. The poem reads, at first, like a meditation on the shallowness of worldly values.

> The Lady Blanch, regardless of all her lover's fears,
> To the Urs'line convent hastens, and long the Abbess hears.
> 'O Blanch, my child, repent ye of the courtly life ye lead!'
> Blanch looked on a rose-bud and little seem'd to heed.
> She looked on the rose-bud, she looked round, and thought
> On all her heart had whisper'd, and all the Nun had taught.
> 'I am worshipped by lovers, and brightly shines my fame,
> All Christendom resoundeth the noble Blanch's name.
> Nor shall I quickly wither like the rose-bud from the tree,
> My queen-like graces shining when my beauty's gone from me.
> But when the sculptur'd marble is raised o'er my head,
> And the matchless Blanch lies lifeless among the noble dead,
> This saintly lady Abbess hath made me justly fear.
> It nothing will avail me that I were worshipp'd here.'

Yet who believes the Abbess and her conventional pieties? There is such relish in the 'queen-like graces', such pleasure in the lovers' worship and the bright fame. The life-denying Abbess could have stepped out of one of the Gothic novels that were currently thrilling the public and it is Blanch, 'the lady of the matchless grace', as Mary called her in another poem, 'Lines on the Same Picture Being Removed to Make Place for a Portrait of a Lady by Titian', who wins the argument here.

'We in these parts are not a little proud of them,' Charles said of these poems. Creatively, Mary's mind often ran in tandem with her brother's. They were both inspired by the Da Vinci print, *The Virgin of the Rocks*. Charles's verse showed the '. . . mother standing by, with trembling passion' watching, uncomprehending as the child John the Baptist: '. . . runs to greet/The greater Infant's feet.' Mary's continued the theme

found in the Blanch poems – male worship of female splen-
dour.

> Maternal lady with the virgin grace,
> Heaven-born thy Jesus seemeth sure,
> And of a virgin pure.
> Lady most perfect, when thy sinless face
> Men look upon, they wish to be
> A Catholic, Madonna fair, to worship thee.

Around this time, she also wrote the poem 'Dialogue Between
a Mother and Child', in which she dramatised and explored
a relationship between parent and son.

CHILD
O Lady, lay your costly robes aside,
No longer may you glory in your pride.

MOTHER
Wherefore to-day are singing in mine ear
Sad songs were made so long ago, my dear;
This day I am to be a bride, you know,
Why sing sad songs, were made so long ago?

CHILD
O mother, lay your costly robes aside,
For you may never be another's bride,
That line I learn'd not in the old sad song.

MOTHER
I pray thee, pretty one, now hold thy tongue,
Play with the bride-maids and be glad, my boy,
For thou shalt be a second father's joy.

CHILD
One father fondled me upon his knee.
One father is enough, alone, for me.

Given Mary's recent history, her troubled relationship with her mother and that relationship's bloody termination, this little elegy is startling. She was writing in the voice of a child who has lost one parent and who feels, unhappily, that he is losing another. There is anger there and menace. But more than that, she was drawing on a popular old song, 'Death and the Lady', in which it is the voice of death that calls on the lady to lay her costly robes aside. In Mary's poem, just as in Mary's life, the child becomes death to the woman.

The small boy attempts to control his world, 'O mother, lay your costly robes aside / For you may never be another's bride,' but is silenced, 'I pray thee, pretty one, now hold thy tongue', as children often are, as Mary certainly was. Yet it is the child's voice that prevails as he flatly refuses to accept another father. From early on, Mary was comfortable adopting a youthful persona in her writing and she was revealing a fascination with the themes of loss and betrayal.

Writing poetry made Mary happy. It was also something she did in order to feel part of her brother's life. On a more prosaic note, she also took up his habit of taking snuff. Their small, white hands, fluttering together over a tortoise-shell snuff box, became, in their friends' eyes, a distinctive image of their intimacy. Charles too was getting his nerve back and beginning to feel more optimistic about their lives. 'We are not placed out of the reach of future interruptions,' he wrote. 'But I am determined to take what snatches of pleasure we can, between the acts of our distressful drama.' They had decided something between them. There was no changing the fact of madness, no shirking the horrible duties it imposed but their lives were not to be entirely grim. By the end of 1800, Charles was less worried about what other people thought; he is going out to dinner, confidently leaving Mary alone to entertain a 'female friend'.

In March of the following year, they moved house again, this time to familiar territory, back to a set of chambers within the Inner Temple. No basement this time, no master above; this time they lived four floors up, in attic rooms with windows that looked out over the River Thames. Moving back to the Temple, back to where they'd grown up, to where their parents had been alive and well, to where they'd once thought they belonged, signalled new hope for both of them. Here they could reclaim what was good in their past and, perhaps, wipe away some of the stain left by the more recent terrible years. Damaged though they had been, they could still start over.

In the summer of 1801, Mary stood up in public, as the bridesmaid at the wedding of an old friend from Temple days. In September, on their first holiday together since childhood, they went to Margate – 'to drink sea water and pick up shells', said Charles. It was such a success that the following year, they went further afield and visited Coleridge in the Lake District. There, they tired themselves climbing hills and drank from cold mountain streams and thrilled to the fine views and then came home and agreed that there was nothing quite as magnificent as London.

They both loved these breaks with routine – typical Londoners, they longed to get away and loved to return to the city. Only Mary's mental relapses were allowed to interfere with their holidays. In March, Mary unexpectedly ran into an old friend of her mother's and it triggered a return of madness. Coleridge was staying with them and witnessed how quickly she could succumb to an attack. 'The Thursday before last she met at Rickman's a Mr Babb an old friend and admirer of her mother. The next day she smiled in an ominous way – on Sunday she told her brother she was getting bad, with great agony – on Tuesday morning she laid hold of me with violent agitation and talked wildly about George Dyer. I told Charles there was not a moment to lose and I did not lose a moment – but went for a hackney coach, and took her to the private madhouse at Hoxton. She was quite calm, and said – it was the best to do so – but she wept bitterly, two or three times, yet all in a calm way.' Yet despite the fear and misery of the attack, she was still able to enjoy a holiday on the Isle of Wight in July, hunting for crabs and borrowing novels from a circulating library.

Slowly, painfully, the brother and sister taught themselves how to manage Mary's illness. Inevitably, the greatest burden fell on her. According to Talfourd, Mary 'experienced, and fully understood premonitory symptoms of the attack. In restlessness, low fever and the inability to sleep.' She learned to watch herself carefully, to study her own mind, to monitor her physical health and she kept her fears secret until the last minute. Coleridge recalled that 'such is the restraining power of her love for Charles Lamb over her mind, that he is always the last person in whose presence any alienation of her understanding betrays itself'. When the signs were too unmistakable to hide, he would be thrown into profound agitation and confusion himself. '. . . When she begins to discover symptoms of approaching illness, it is not easy to say what is best to do,' he once confided in Dorothy Wordsworth. 'Being by ourselves is bad, and going out is bad. I get so irritable and wretched with fear, that I constantly hasten on the disorder.' Knowing that she would be ill and have to leave him made him 'little better than light-headed'.

So Mary involved Charles only when she knew she had no other option and she tried to spare him pain when she asked for his help. Talfourd wrote that, 'as gently as possible, she prepared her brother for the duty he must soon perform.' Charles then asked for a day off work, she packed her strait-jacket and together they went to the asylum where he would leave her until she recovered. Charles Lloyd once met them as they were walking there; they were both crying. It is an unbearably sad image and it haunted everyone who knew the Lambs. Years later, Valentine le Grice recalled the scene in the verse, 'Hand Clasped in Hand':

> An angel's wing is wavering o'er their heads,
> While they, the brother and the sister walk:
> Nor dare, as heedless of its fanning, talk
> Of woes which are not buried with the dead
>
> Hand clasped in hand they move; adown their cheeks
> From the full heart-spring, tears o'erflowing gush;
> Close and more close they clasp, as if to speak
> Would wake the sorrows which they seek to hush.
>
> Down to the mansion slow their footsteps tend,
> Where blank despair is soothed by mercy's spell;
> Pausing in momentary pray'r to bend,
>
> Ere the cheered sister passes to her cell.
> Soon in the hope that yet there will be given
> Calm and sweet hours – foretastes of heaven.

Without her, Charles was lost, 'like a fool, bereft of her co-operation. I dare not think, lest I should think wrong; so used am I to look up to her in the least and the biggest perplexity.' He thought she was 'older and wiser and better than him' and he often blamed himself for her relapses, accusing himself of 'wasting and teasing her life' with his 'cursed drinking and ways of going on'.

His heavy drinking (he was once put in the stocks after a bout of drunken carousing), the warning symptoms, the sudden fear, the sad walks, the wretched separations, guilt and unhappiness – these things were to be part of the Lambs' lives but they were not, they determined, to be the only things. In the years immediately following their father's death, they set up the pattern of their lives together. They would both write. By the end of 1803, Charles had started writing articles for the *Morning Post* and had already finished two plays, *Rosamund Gray* and *John Woodvill*, both of which had been refused by theatres but which he liked enough to have published at his own cost. For Mary, there would be periods in the asylum, but there would also be holidays, long unfettered hikes up mountains and the freshness of sea air. She would know isolation and loneliness but she would also have intimacy and close friendships. And her greatest friendship, the one with Sarah Stoddart, would help shape her thinking in such a way that it would enable her to write her best book, *Tales from Shakespeare*.

Chapter 7

Always the Bridesmaid

When madness exists in the blood of families, and shews itself regular in the several branches of the pedigree, ill-concerted alliances will always keep up the general tendency to the disease. What then shall be said of those, who either from ambitious or lucrative motives, stifle the feelings of honour and humanity, and sordidly submit to form connections which entail miseries on their posterity, more grievous than death itself: Such matrimonial contracts, therefore should be avoided, and, if possible, prevented by everyone who is a well-wisher to society: indeed, I feel no reluctance whatever, in pronouncing those who engage in, and those who encourage and promote such alliances, to be, in the strictest sense, enemies to their country.

William Pargeter MD, *Observations on Maniacal Disorder*, 1792

FOR MARY, MARRIAGE AND children were not to be thought of. There was a widespread belief among doctors that madness was hereditary and, now that she knew that her own particular illness was likely to be recurring, she recognised that her life was

91

going to be single and childless. Charles came to the same conclusion; he once described his lot in life as the 'perpetual prospect of celibacy', but they responded to the inevitable in different ways. Charles always protested – too much perhaps? – that the single life suited him, claiming that 'there is a quiet dignity in old-bachelorhood, a leisure from cares, noise &c, and enthronization upon the armed-chair of a man's feelings that he may sit, walk, read, unmolested, to none accountable'.

He compared his relationship with Mary against the model of matrimony and found that it measured up. Shortly after the death of his mother, he wrote to Coleridge that he was 'wedded to the fortunes' of his sister. Refusing, on Mary's behalf, an invitation to go and convalesce with Coleridge and his wife, he declared that he, Charles, was the best companion for her and declared it in language borrowed from the lexicon of courtship. 'I know a young man,' he wrote, 'who has suited her these twenty years and may live to do so still – if we are one day restor'd to each other.' When Mary was away from home, separated from her brother by one of her frequent bouts of madness, he wrote of himself as a 'widow'd thing'.

Charles credited Mary with feeling exactly as he did. 'She would share life and death, heaven and hell with me,' he told Dorothy Wordsworth and then, adapting the words of the marriage service, 'She lives but for me . . . she has cleaved to me for better, for worse.' Mary, however, never spoke or wrote of her relationship with her brother as if it was a substitute for marriage. She understood clearly what she was missing and consoled herself by an intense involvement in the affairs of others. 'Like all old maids I feel a mighty solicitude about the event of love stories,' she said of herself. She delighted in the birth of her friends' babies and when an infant died, her sympathy was prompt and profound. She was loving and interested in their children as they grew up and, according to Mary Cowden Clarke, one of her Latin pupils and little favourites, 'She had a most tender sympathy for the young.' Cowden Clarke recalled how Mary 'entered into their juvenile ideas with a tact and skill quite surprising. She threw herself so entirely into their way of thinking, and contrived to take an estimate of things so completely from their point of view, that she made them rejoice to have her for their co-mate in affairs that interested them.'

In Sarah Stoddart, Mary found not only a good and close friend but also the perfect outlet for her feelings on the forbidden topic of marriage. It was Mary's opinion that 'next to the pleasure of being married, is the pleasure of making, or helping marriages forward', and Sarah was determined to get married. The two women met sometime in the summer of 1802 – their brothers were friends – and quickly struck up an intimacy that pleased and satisfied both their needs.

Sarah Stoddart was the daughter of a half pay naval lieutenant in charge of press-ganging. She had lived most of her life at Winterslow near Salisbury, apart from time at boarding school and months she spent on extended holidays at friends' houses. She was intelligent: she could read and write French and had a made a study of botany, taking Rousseau for a guide. As some of her letters to an old schoolfriend, Sophie Haytor, show, she enjoyed inventing and solving acrostics. Her grandson, William Carew Hazlitt, writing in a memoir of his family, said Sarah was 'endowed with no ordinary intelligence and information'. She was always borrowing books and was 'a person, indeed, of extraordinary reading, and what she read she kept'. She liked the novels of Sir Walter Scott and the poetry of Byron and Wordsworth. Her nephew said she was 'a remarkable and learned woman, and one whose society was sought'.

The Stoddart family were richer than the Lambs – there was a private income as well as the father's naval salary and Sarah had some money of her own – but they were not as socially established as some of its members would have liked. They were status conscious and snobbish, preoccupied with social climbing. Her brother John was delighted when his Cambridge college had 'nine noblemen, which is one more than last term'. His many letters to her contained as much advice as they did affection. He was approving when Sarah was introduced to a Lady Heathcote: 'such connections will be a source of credit and satisfaction to you,' he noted and later he was equally pleased that she was able to 'keep up an intimacy' with a Miss Walter and a Mrs Roberts. 'It is well,' he wrote, 'to be on good terms with every body particularly in a genteel style.' Her mother was equally pressing with her advice; when Sarah was away on a visit, she wrote to warn her against excess, imploring her 'not to be tempted by the plenty you see around you and the hospitality with which, as visitor, you will be treated, to indulge more in eating, drinking and amusement than is right.' It was better, she went on, to act diffident than to fall 'into a contrary excess, than which nothing is more disgusting and disagreeable in a female character'.

Sarah though was something of a free sprit. She cut her hair short and said yes please when her father offered her some of his grog. 'Not that she ever indulged to excess but she was that sort of woman,' her Victorian grandson observed primly. 'She hated formality and etiquette,' he went on. She once laughingly described one of her nephews (the son of her far more stiff-mannered brother) as being like 'an old-fashioned dancing master'. When an old schoolfriend of her brother's – someone she had known well enough to address by his Christian name – succeeded to the peerage, her shocked relatives stopped her from writing him a letter using the old familiar name. To her contemporaries she was a hoyden. Even Mary Lamb, no genteel lady herself, told her that she had 'a total want of politeness in behaviour' and lacked both self-respect and 'a certain dignity of action' but she said it with affection and she warmed to Sarah's frankness and lack of pretension.

Sarah had her own role to play in her family's game of elegant go-getting and she did her best except when more commonplace pleasures got in the way. To read her correspondence is like living the raw materials of a Jane Austen novel, stepping into a world of determinedly maintained respectability, morning calls, agreeable amusements, new connections and, above all, beaux. The aim of all this self-regulation and cultivating of good company was, of course, marriage. By the time she met Mary, Sarah had already tried and failed to marry several men. Her primary assistant in this husband hunt was a Mrs Parsons who lived in Fulham and, in return for Sarah's help nursing a sick husband, conspired and plotted with her to introduce her to suitable men. This 'truly valuable good friend', as Mrs Stoddart called her, tried to fix Sarah up with a Mr Read but it came to nothing, despite Sarah's father praising her 'amiable disposition and good qualities fitted to make a man happy, who was fond of a domestic life'. Her mother, however, thought Sarah was well out of it: 'Think of the horror of being tied to a splenetic old man, buried alive in the prime of your life.' A Mr Warren didn't come up to scratch because her fortune was too small and a nephew of the Reverend Parson, who was professing 'to be looking out for a wife', couldn't look in the direction of Sarah because he could 'think of none under 10 thousand pounds'. All these failed courtships were carried on in the full view and with the enthusiastic support of the whole Stoddart family. Sarah also indulged in a private intrigue all her own, carrying on a secret correspondence with a young Cambridge friend of her brother's, a piece of forwardness that, when discovered, drew the sternest censure from her mother, dismayed at her 'improper conduct'.

She was twenty-seven when she met Mary Lamb and cynical as only someone who had been wheeling and dealing in the marriage market could be. Her parents were getting on in years and she had to look after them, taking care of her father's laundry and worrying over her mother's health. When she visited the Parsons, she was fixed there until her brother John found the time to come and take her home. Like Mary, she knew just how much drudgery landed on the shoulders of an unmarried daughter. She yearned for independence and no doubt thought she would have more as a wife than as a daughter and a sister. Despite her illness, Mary – as Charles's companion, housekeeper and soon-to-be writing partner – had the better deal. But, barring the pressure to get married, Mary had stood in Sarah's shoes and found them just as uncomfortable.

The two women had a lot in common. They both loved reading and gossip, and enjoyed a little brandy and hot water – 'three parts brandy to one part water' was Mary's recipe. Both were skilled at sewing; when they knew each other well, Sarah was generous in making clothes for Mary while the older woman ran her London errands, such as enquiring about Sarah's mother's pension. Sarah took a keen interest in fashion – her ongoing attempts to find a husband meant she had to keep up appearances – but her method was erratic and the results eccentric. In one letter, her mother expressed concern at how few clothes Sarah had taken with her on a visit. 'You must be almost as unclothed as your grandmother Eve,' she wrote. 'I admire your disregard of finery – but don't go naked.' Sarah's grandson described her as 'destitute of all taste in dress'. He repeats an anecdote from a lady visited by Sarah one wet day. 'She was dressed in a white muslin gown, a black velvet spencer, and a leghorn hat with a white feather. Her clothes were perfectly saturated, and a complete change of things was necessary, before she could sit down.' Sarah's brother nagged her about her appearance, advising that 'we should equally abstain from coarseness, rusticity and vulgarity . . . In dress for instance, everyone is pleas'd to see a simplicity and neatness, but there is a way of putting on the simplest garment which will make it sit with ease and give a graceful appearance to the whole frame; on the other hand the material of the dress may be plain and neat enough, and yet ill form or manner of adjustment may make the wearer look like a dowdy. These slight hints I merely throw out for your imagination to work upon . . .'

Mary took to Sarah immediately. Shortly after their meeting, sometime in 1802, she wrote to her – the first of Mary's letters that still exists – beginning formally, addressing her as 'My dear Miss Stoddart' – and apologising for not having replied to her letter sooner. Within a few lines though, she was stating clearly her wish to know her friend better. 'I am always a miserable letter writer, and I feel the want, in writing to a new friend of being able to talk of the days "O lang syne": but this is a defect I trust time will remedy.' She longed to see her again. 'The evenings we spent together were the pleasantest I have known for a very long time,' she wrote and she already appreciated how difficult it was for Sarah to get away from home. 'I fear you have somehow procured a false character to obtain permission to return to us. I will with pleasure sign any paper of that kind you may have occasion for.' She was the older woman, writing a report on the younger. 'I will protest you are the most amusing, good-humoured, good sister, and altogether excellent girl I know, or any other fibs you will please to dictate to me.'

From there, she moved to general chitchat, remarks about Charles who had an eye infection, remembrances to a lady whose name Mary had forgotten, polite references to Sarah Stoddart's parents. She signed herself 'I will ever be your affectionate friend' and the postscript begged 'write soon'.

It was not until December that Mary wrote to Sarah again – in between there was a holiday with Coleridge in the Lake District and a return of her illness – but when she took up her pen, her thoughts of Sarah and her liking for her were as keen as ever; the letter was full of 'the memory of our walks together – driving along the Strand so fast . . . returning home in all haste, to be scolded for not laying the cloth in time for supper (albeit it being nine o'clock) and then chidden for laughing in an unseemly manner. I have never half liked being at your brothers' room since you left them: – they sit and preach about learned matters, while I turn over an old book, and when I am weary look in the window in the corner where you and your work-bag used to be, and wish for you to rout them up and make us all alive.'

Mary found Sarah's company stimulating. Eleven years younger than herself, Sarah's future was still unsettled and she attacked her prospects with an exuberance that amused, amazed and excited Mary. For Mary men were not, never had been, never would be possible suitors but her letters to Sarah Stoddart show how easily she could sympathise with the conventional hopes and aspirations of a marriageable woman and how much she felt she was missing out on. Once, when writing about the gift of a pin from Sarah's brother, she added somewhat skittishly, 'never having had any presents from gentlemen in my young days, I highly prize all they now give me, thinking my latter days are better than my former.' Her correspondence with Sarah Stoddart – twenty-three letters still exist – shed a revealing light on some of the secrets locked up in Mary's heart, exposing the nature and depth of her feelings about romantic love and relationships, feelings which, due to her illness, were always to be thwarted. Mary needed experiences to share just as Sarah needed a confidante with whom to share them.

Mary Lamb's Quaker dress and mild manner were misleading, causing observers and biographers to categorise her as a sexless creature, devoid of passion and only interested in the care and support of her brother. She *was* a devoted sister but she was also the woman who, in her middle age, responded to the news that the Queen, Caroline of Brunswick, had been accused of adultery with the open-minded view that 'I should not think the better of her, if I were sure she was what is called innocent.' She was also the woman who, during a light-hearted party game on the subject of 'persons one would wish to have seen', picked Ninon de L'Enclos, a fantastically sexy French courtesan, so unalterably beautiful that rumour whispered she had sold her soul to the devil in return for a secret youth-preserving potion. Ninon had been advised by her father on his deathbed to get as much fun as possible out of life and obeyed him by first eloping with a young prince and then taking a series of lovers that included Cardinal Richelieu, the Duke of St Évremond and Rochefoucauld. 'Men lose more conquests by their own awkwardness than by any virtue in the woman,' Ninon once quipped.

In Mary's mad moments, she reminded her listeners of Congreve. She might have been self-effacing, quiet and modest most of the time but, somewhere within her, lurked a Millamant, witty, charming, sexually confident and sought after. She wrote poetry about desirable women, about the Lady Blanch reluctantly repenting of her triumphs over men and another about Salome: 'Fair Salome, who did excel / All in that land for dancing well' who 'fired' a 'feastful monarch's heart' and brought about the death of John the Baptist.

Mary was more than capable of responding to men. 'I have known many single men I should have liked in my life (if it had suited them) for a husband,' she wrote in one of her letters to Sarah. And she had an unused store of love and generosity. When Sarah was worrying over the details of a marriage settlement, Mary told her: 'If I had been blessed with a good fortune, and that marvellous blessing to boot a husband I verily believe I should have crammed it all uncounted into his pocket.'

Who were these single men who she would have liked for a husband? There were plenty of candidates because Charles had many friends and Mary knew most of them and some very well. She was fond of George Dyer who was nine years older than herself. He had been at Christ's Hospital too, but long before her brother. He was very like Charles, dressed in the same clerical style of black knee breeches, black stockings (Charles covered his with black gaiters) and black shoes. Dyer also had a hesitating way of speaking, filling in the gaps with a little monosyllable: abd-abd-abd – rather like Charles's stutter. Her brother adored him: 'God never put a kinder heart into flesh of man than George Dyer's,' he said. Dyer was a prolific journalist and writer and a bad poet. He was poor but extravagantly generous, once giving his stagecoach fare to an impoverished friend and then walking all the way from London to Cambridge himself. Absent-minded – on one occasion he took off one of his shoes at someone's house and then walked out without noticing his foot was bare. He was so sweet and forgetful, so kind and so shabbily dressed that he cried out to be looked after. Mary and Sarah once took pity on his tatty old armchair and sewed up all the holes in it only to discover he had packed each hole with books. Mary raved about him during a period of mania. She took an active interest in his love life; at one point she and Charles convinced him to pay court to Elizabeth Benger but it came to nothing as the novelist wasn't interested. Southey said the Lambs had got Dyer into a 'quagmire and cannot get him out again, for they have failed in the attempt to talk Miss Bungay or Bungey or Benjey into love with him'.

Thomas Manning was another of Mary's favourites. Described by a mutual friend as a 'darling of Mary Lamb's', Manning was the son of a rector of Diss in Norfolk. He knew a great deal about Mary, having been the recipient of many of Charles's agonised letters about her illness. He was playful, liking to pull faces and make puns. He sent gifts of game to Charles and encouraged him in his writing. A mathematician, linguist and traveller, his particular passion was China; he went to study there in 1806. 'We shall miss him very much, for he has been very much with us lately, and we love him dearly,' wrote Mary. She was deeply upset when he left without saying a proper goodbye. From China, he sent her gifts of silk. When he was due to return, nearly ten years later, Charles wrote him: 'Mary reserves a portion of your silk . . . to make up spick and span into a new-bran gown to wear when you come.'

Mary got on well with men, being unjudgmental, a good listener and the possessor of an excellent recipe for strong punch – 'deceitfully strong', Coleridge called it. Her system for man management was simple – leave them alone, she told Sarah Stoddart. 'I make a point of conscience never to interfere, or cross my brother in the humour he happens to be in. It always seems to me to be a vexatious kind of tyranny that women have no business to exercise over men, which merely because *they having a better judgement* they have the power to do. Leave *men* alone, and at last we find they come round to the right way, which we by a kind of intuition perceive at once. But better, far better, that we should let them often do wrong, than that they should have the torment of a Monitor always at their elbows.' However, it was a married man not a single one for whom she cared most deeply. This was Coleridge. She had known him for years and, because he had long been her brother's closest friend, she had seen the best of him, and the best of Coleridge was wonderful. Another Christ's Hospital boy, the radical journalist Leigh Hunt described Coleridge as 'a mighty intellect put upon a sensual body . . . very metaphysical and very corporeal'. The combination was irresistible.

Samuel Taylor Coleridge by Peter Vandyke.

He amused and distressed her in equal measure. The only letter of hers to him that still exists began: 'I have read your silly very silly letter and between laughing and crying I hardly know how to answer it. You are too serious and too kind a vast deal, for we are not much used to either seriousness or kindness from our present friends and therefore your letter has put me into a greater hurry of spirits that your pleasant Segar did last night.' Coleridge's own behaviour was often so erratic that, in another age, he might well have been diagnosed with manic depression himself. His extremes of mirth and melancholy, his swinging between gravity and sweetness, set off a response in her that was both exciting and uncomfortable.

People close to Mary saw how Coleridge disturbed her. Charles told him, 'You have a power of exciting interest, of leading all hearts captive, too forcible to admit of Mary's being with you – I consider her as perpetually on the brink of madness – I think, you would almost make her dance within an inch of the precipice – she must be with duller fancies and cooler intellects.' William Hazlitt too thought Coleridge's presence upset Mary and Henry Crabb Robinson, a barrister and diarist and a particularly involved and detailed describer of the Lamb household, directly attributed at least one of her attacks of madness to the fact that Coleridge had been staying with them. Coleridge's company, he observed, 'has a dreadful effect upon her nerves and shatters her frame. The conversation of such a man, whose eloquence is full of passion and mystical philosophy, a compound of poetry, metaphysics, plaintive egotism and diseased sensibility, continued for hours to a late hour in the night, is enough to disorder a sane but susceptible frame, much more rouse a dormant disease of imagination.' But Mary also affected Coleridge. Once when Mary was ill – 'overset' – was his phrase, he became unwell too. The death of a mutual friend, George Burnett, 'told too abruptly, and in truth, exaggerated, overset my dear, most dear, and most excellent friend and heart's sister Mary Lamb – and her illness has almost overset me'. Mary raved to Mrs Godwin that she was frightened that Coleridge was unhinged, she wrote to William Wordsworth, begging him to come to London to rescue him.

Coleridge was a worry to all his friends. Mary fretted over him as opium addiction wrecked his mental and physical health. She exchanged updates on his condition with Dorothy Wordsworth who seemed to be as powerfully affected by Coleridge as she was herself. The 'fatigue' of his conversation brought on 'low spirits' in Mary and she experienced 'anxious care even to misery' as she contemplated him. She loved his two sons, called the youngest by his pet name, always enquired after their health and bought them books. She knew a great deal – perhaps too much for her peace of mind – about his miserable relationship with his wife and, on at least one occasion, it became her responsibility to write letters to Sarah Coleridge informing her of her errant husband's whereabouts. She insisted he kept in touch with his wife but she also wanted to see the letters. 'You must positively must write to Mrs Coleridge this day, and you must write here that I may know you write or you must come and dictate a letter for me to write to her,' she once instructed him. When Coleridge's marriage to Sarah looked particularly difficult, her restraint left her and she wrote to Dorothy Wordsworth suggesting that anyone who had influence should use it to bring about a separation, a letter she instantly regretted and longed to recall. 'I feel it very wrong in me even in the remotest degree to do anything to prevent her seeing that husband – she and her husband being the only people who ought to be concerned in the affair.' She was especially anxious that Charles did not know that she had written 'something improper'. She was hurt and angry when she thought Coleridge was slighting her brother and herself. 'We expect too much and he gives too little.'

Coleridge cared deeply about Mary in return, describing her as his 'dear, most dear, and most excellent friend and heart's sister'. She was like 'an only sister' to him. He appreciated her intelligence and her affectionate nature: 'Her mind is elegantly stored – her heart feeling.' He had been willing to share the responsibility for her medical care, offering Charles money towards her madhouse fees and he was a close enough friend to have seen her in the grip of rising mania. He turned to her when he was unhappy; when his quarrel with William Wordsworth almost broke his heart, he arrived at her home, his face wild and pale and sobbed out his misery into her listening and loving ears. But Coleridge was married. That he was unhappily married probably only made things worse. There is nothing quite as dangerous to a single woman's peace of mind as an unhappily married man with whom she is on affectionate and intimate terms.

That in Mary, Sarah found the perfect listener for her marriage plans, tells us as much about Mary's own desires as it does about Sarah's. She loved Sarah's letters, telling her two years after their meeting: 'Your letters my dear Sarah are to me very, very precious ones, they are the kindest, best, most natural ones I ever received.' The mentor always gets as much out of the relationship as the protégée and Mary thrilled to Sarah's vivacity. By killing her mother, Mary had so thoroughly violated society's laws that, for ever afterwards, she felt she had to keep a guard on her wilder self and she so managed herself that the impression she gave was of a quiet, calm, well-behaved and modest woman. Yet she could easily relate to Sarah, this bold-acting woman of spirit who declared her desires and acted on them. No wonder she loved her and loved her with a protecting love; it was her own unfulfilled self she was sheltering. In her letters, though, Mary did not try to identify with Sarah; she was wiser and kinder than that. She allowed her to be her own woman. 'The terms you are upon with your Lover does (as you say it will) appear wondrous strange to me, however, as I cannot enter into your feelings, I certainly can have nothing to say to it, only that I sincerely wish you happy in your way, however odd that way may appear to me to be. I would begin now to advise you to drop all correspondence with William, but, as I said before, as I cannot enter into your feelings, and views of things, your ways not being my ways, why should I tell you what I would do in your situation. So child take thy own ways and God prosper thee in them.' Sarah opened her heart to Mary, receiving in return, an affectionate interest that must have been gratifying, comforting and flattering.

Mary listened to the young woman, praised her, scolded her, advised and saw the best in her. 'I love you for the good that is in you, and look for no change,' she writes. She entered wholeheartedly into Sarah's adventures. When Sarah went to join her brother in Malta where he had been made Judge Advocate and Coleridge followed soon after, Mary followed them both in spirit. 'We talk; but it is but wild and idle talk of following him: he is to get my brother some little snug place of a thousand a year, and we are to leave all, and come and live among ye – what a pretty dream.'

In imagination, she accompanied her friend into 'the first bustle of a new reception, every moment seeing new faces, and staring at new objects...gay, splendid doings.' Sarah made fresh conquests and Mary listened to the account of her love adventures with amusement and pleasure. 'I thank you for your frank communication and, I beg you will continue it in future ... You surprise and please me with the frank and generous way in which you deal with your lovers, taking a refusal from their cold prudential hearts, with a better grace, and more good humour than other women accept a suitor's service.'

She entrusted her beloved Coleridge to Sarah and Sarah's family. 'Be to him kind and affectionate nurses and mind now that you perform this duty faithfully, and write me a good account of yourself. Behave to him as you would to me, or to Charles if we came sick and unhappy to you.'

Poor Sarah did not spend long in Malta. The manners which were a little too free and easy even by English standards were hopelessly unsuited to a small island. She had trouble fitting in and there is a suggestion that she became embroiled in a scandal, probably even ran into physical danger from a man. Mary sympathised with her 'distresses' in Malta and suggested that she was always unlikely to 'flourish in a little proud Garrison Town.' She was angry that her friend had received an 'insult . . . from a vile wretch there'. When she learned that John Stoddart was annoyed that his sister had yet to become a 'fine lady', Mary mocked his pretensions by joking that such a role was easy enough to fake, 'I have observed many a demure lady who passes muster admirably well who I think we could easily learn to imitate in a week or two.'

However, the main reason Sarah returned home was to take care of her mother who had become mentally ill and who had been placed in an asylum. Madness and the care of a sick mother were two subjects Mary understood well and her letters were full of sympathy. She knew, none could know better, what both mother and daughter were suffering. 'I have entered very deeply into your affliction with regard to your Mother,' she writes. 'I speak from experience and from the opportunity I have had of much observation in such cases that insane people in the fancy's they take into their heads do not feel as one in a sane state of mind does.' All the wisdom culled so painfully from her own experience came out as she encouraged Sarah not to let herself be too deeply affected by her mother's 'unhappy malady' and to get away whenever she could. 'I do not think your own presence necessary unless she takes to you very much except for the purpose of seeing with your own eyes that she is very kindly treated.' Mary had found to her cost, to her life-long cost, just how terrible can be the duty of care imposed on a daughter, and wanted to see her friend spared the same ordeal.

Mary's home became a bolt-hole for Sarah. She stayed with her for several weeks at the beginning of 1806; on her departure, Mary wrote, expressing her sympathy for the 'dull prospect' before her. She offered her an open invitation: 'Whenever you feel yourself disposed to run away from your troubles, come to us again,' and 'I think I should like to have you always to the end of our lives living with us, and I do not know any reason why that should not be except for the great fancy you seem to have for marrying, which after all is but a hazardous kind of an affair, but however do as you like, every man knows best what pleases himself best.'

In return, Sarah offered Mary a different sort of escape, a place where she could unload some of her troubling feelings about herself and her brother. Throughout the previous winter, she had struggled badly with low spirits and confessed them to Sarah. She tried to alter her 'fretful temper to a calm and quiet one'. If willpower alone could master clinical depression, Mary would do it: 'I am most seriously intending to bend the whole force of my mind to counteract this, and I think I see some prospect of success.'

Although Mary and Charles loved each other, they irritated each other. Charles feared that his drinking sometimes drove Mary into madness and she, in turn, aggravated his always volatile moods. 'When I am pretty well his low spirits throws me back again and when he begins to get a little cheerful then

I do the same kind office for him,' is how Mary summed up this uncomfortable see-saw ride. 'You would laugh, or you would cry, perhaps both, to see us sit together looking at each other with long and rueful faces, and saying how do you do? And how do you do? And then we fall a crying and say we will be better on the morrow – he says we are like tooth ache and his friend gum bile, which though a kind of ease, is but an uneasy kind of ease, a comfort of rather an uncomfortable sort.'

Mary told Sarah about her depressions but asked her not to mention that she had done so to Charles. It will 'vex' him was her explanation but she also wanted to keep some secrets just between her and her friend. She and Charles were short of money and one solution would have been to leave London for somewhere they could live much more cheaply but Mary knew there was a limit to how much of each other's company they could bear. 'Till I do find we really are comfortable alone, and by ourselves, it seems a dangerous experiment,' she wrote. In happy moods, she recognised that she and Charles were the mainstay, the support and anchor of each other's lives. On bad days, things looked very bleak. 'Our love has been the torment of our lives hitherto,' she told Sarah.

Overnight stays with the Lambs were welcome but Sarah was still desperate to get married. Mary heard all about a Mr White and a Mr Turner and a Mr Dowling who was an ill-educated farmer much younger than Sarah. In the end, Sarah married Charles Lamb's friend, the critic and essayist William Hazlitt. On the face of it, it wasn't too bad a match. Neither of them pretended to be wildly in love but both were ready to find each other acceptable, Sarah, if only to get away from her home situation, and Hazlitt was always susceptible to women. He was poor, managing to get by on the occasional portrait commission – he had yet to find his voice as an essayist

– and loans from good-natured friends. Therefore he could be expected not to have the sort of raised expectations regarding settlements that some of Sarah's previous, more worldly suitors had. He was eight years younger than she was but they were both intelligent and well read and he was unconventional enough himself not to mind Sarah's unorthodox behaviour. He suspected but did not seem to mind that she was 'no maid'. They met at the Lambs' and by the summer of 1807 things between them were proceeding very well. Mary entered into the affair wholeheartedly – 'if your determination be to have him, heaven send you many happy years together' she wrote to her friend and she begged to be shown Hazlitt's love letters. Yet the love affair also puzzled her. She called it 'comical' and once declared that she would like to see Sarah and Hazlitt 'come together, if (as Charles observes) it were only for the joke's sake'.

There was a suggestion of doubt beneath Mary's good wishes. 'I now mean not only to hope, and wish, but to persuade myself that you will be very happy together.' Nevertheless she was bridesmaid when they married on 1 May 1808 at St Andrew's Church after making an uncharacteristically girlish fuss about whether to wear a sprigged muslin gown or run up a new silk one. She was too poor to give them a wedding present but went to the wedding, she said, 'with a willing mind, bringing nothing with me but many wishes, and not a few hopes, and a very little of fears – of happy years to come'. Did Mary know that St Andrew's, Holborn, was the church where her mother's funeral had taken place? Charles knew and perhaps it was that as much as the oddity of the union which made him see a grim humour in the service. Years later, he wrote: 'I was at Hazlitt's marriage and had like to have been turned out several times during the ceremony. Any thing awful makes me laugh. I misbehaved once at a funeral.'

The Lambs continued to see the Hazlitts after the wedding, marshalling their finances carefully so as to afford a visit to Winterslow and entertaining them in London. Both couples were poor and Mary and Sarah conspired to keep Hazlitt from knowing that his guests were contributing to their keep. Martin Burney came with them in the summer of 1809 and slept on the floor; 'he and I have calculated that if he has no Inn-expenses he may as well spare that money, to give you for a part of his roast beef. We can spare you also just five pounds. You are not to say this to Hazlitt lest his delicacy should be alarmed.' The holiday was a

William Hazlitt by John Hazlitt.

success; Mary wrote one of her happiest, most lyrical letters afterwards – 'the dear quiet lazy delicious month we spent with you', she enthused; it was a visit made especially pleasant as it came after a particularly bad episode of madness. The Lambs had moved house again, and the upheaval had had its usual effect. Still, she was able to relish her holiday with her friend; 'I never passed such a pleasant time in the country in my life, both in the house and out of it – the card playing quarrels, and a few gaspings for breath, after your swift footsteps up the high hills excepted.'

However the Stoddart/Hazlitt marriage was pretty miserable: the couple were totally unsuited. Their grandson wrote of them: 'Never, I suppose, was there a worse assorted pair than my grandfather and grandmother.' Although he maintained that 'if they had not happened to marry, if they had continued to meet at the Lambs; as of old, or at her brothers, they would have remained the best of friends,' he was also convinced that Hazlitt was actually disgusted by Sarah. 'I should even go so far as to say that he had his individual case and fate in view, where he speaks of marriages being brought abut sometimes 'by repugnance and a sort of fatal fascinating.' For their censorious Victorian grandson, the fault was Sarah's. 'We know that apart from any merely sentimental and transitory attachments he may have formed, he was disappointed in love at an early age, in a manner which preyed upon his spirits afterwards, and that he never thoroughly rallied from the blow. Added to all this, he was induced to enter into a marriage which was certainly not one of choice (though it was no in way forced upon him), and the woman with whom he thus knit himself permanently was one of the least domestic of her sex. She was a lady of excellent disposition, an affectionate mother, and endowed with no ordinary intelligence and infor- mation. But for household economy she had not the slightest turn; and she was selfish, unsympathizing, without an idea of management, and destitute of all taste in dress.'

Poor Sarah Stoddart. Hers was a hard life; she suffered many miscarriages and two of her children died in infancy. Mary was a constant friend throughout, consoling her on her losses, congratulating her from a full and loving heart on the birth of the one boy who survived – 'I never knew an event of the kind that gave me so much pleasure as the little-long-looked- for-come-at-last's arrival, and I rejoiced to hear his honour has begun to suck,' she wrote joyously.

Sarah's marriage collapsed when Hazlitt fell obsessively in love with another woman – a passion he described in *Liber Amoris* – and asked for a divorce, which she granted. The divorce was a partly comic, wholly bizarre set-up in which the two of them had to travel to Scotland at the same time but not together and tell all manner of lies to the authorities. Mary was disgusted on Sarah's behalf, though her friend seemed prepared to enjoy her life as a newly single woman. Over the years, as she saw friends like Sarah suffer in marriage, Mary came to see that the single life, while it meant the absence of a certain kind of passion, also meant the absence of certain kinds of grief. When another friend lost a child, Mary wrote with feeling, 'I am glad I am an old maid, for you see there is nothing but misfortunes in the marriage state.' Seeing Sarah's distresses helped her appreciate her own contentment but the old maid's taste for matchmaking had allowed her to see the intricate rituals of courtship close up and appreciate the heat and energy of the sex hunt. That knowledge lodged itself in her imagination until she was ready to use it in her writing. For Mary Lamb, it was fictionalised love, theatrical love, Shakespearean love that she was to make her own and, in the end, that love was more lasting than her friend's marriage.

21 July 1802   Temple

My dear Miss Stoddart

              I am ashamed of having your kind
letter so long by me unanswered: it lies upon the table
and reproaches me all day long — when I begged you
would write to me, I forgot to inform you — I am much
fonder of receiving letters, than writing them: but I
believe this is no very uncommon case. Charles received
a letter from your brother the same day I did yours, and
the one neglected to answer it till yesterday, when after
writing and burning a dozen sheets of paper (which perhaps
you do not know is his usual habit) he sent your brother
a little short nothing-at-all-about letter of six lines: as
I shall do you. I am always a miserable letter, writer and I
feel the want, in writing to a new friend of being able to
talk of the days "lang syne": but this is a defect I
trust time will remedy.
I am very glad the waistcoats puzzled you, you were so proud
you would not let me do them: I intend when your brother

Chapter 8

Round Unvarnished Tales

Love's a mighty lord,
And hath so humbled me as I confess
There is no woe to his correction,
Nor to his service no such joy on earth.
Now no discourse, except it be of love;
Now can I break my fast, dine, sup, and sleep,
Upon the very naked name of love
    The Two Gentlemen of Verona,
    William Shakespeare, c. 1592

Love is a mighty lord, and hath so humbled me, that
I confess there is no woe like his correction, nor no
such joy on earth as in his service. I now like no
discourse except it be of love. Now I can break my
fast, dine, sup, and sleep, upon the very name of love
    'The Two Gentlemen of Verona',
    Tales from Shakespeare, Mary Lamb, 1807

IN FEBRUARY 1806, MARY SAT down and, with a rising sense
of energy and purpose, wrote a new kind of letter to Sarah
Stoddart. 'I am going to make a sort of a promise to myself
and to you that, I will write you kind of journal-like letters,

of the daily what-we-do-matters, as they occur.' As well as writing to a friend, she was also setting herself a literary exercise, playing with the epistolary form, a narrative device that had been used very successfully by best-selling author Fanny Burney in her 1778 novel, *Evelina*.

Literature was uppermost in Mary Lamb's mind. She badly wanted to write. Her brother was still thinking about writing plays; at the beginning of 1806, he rented a room outside their apartment where he could be alone to work on his new project, a farce. Mary saw his absence as a chance to get some work done herself. 'Charles has left me for the first time to go to his lodgings . . .' she told Sarah '. . . and I am holding a solitary consultation with myself, as to how I shall employ myself.' So far, she had only written a few verses but now there was a new energy in her thinking. 'Writing plays, novels, poems, and all manner of such-like vapourings and vapourish schemes are floating in my head.'

It took some time for these vapourish schemes to harden. Mary's writing was always sandwiched between domestic duties. As well as the writing schemes, she was also thinking about making a new gown and wondering if perhaps she should use the time to do some ironing. And Charles's farce took precedence over anything she might write. His experiment with solitude was a disaster: the following night he stayed home, declaring he needed a holiday from writing. He was restless, demanding so much of her time and attention that she barely had time to write her letter, let alone anything else. 'We have talked and thought about nothing but the farce night and day,' she explained to Sarah Stoddart and added, with sisterly loyalty, 'I like it very much and cannot help having great hopes of its success.' It was called *Mr H* and Mary took the manuscript to Richard Wroughton, the actor/manager at Drury Lane Theatre. He promised nothing more than giving the play to the theatre owner to read, leaving the Lambs still on tenterhooks.

For the next few weeks, Mary was unable to get down to any work. Charles was so unsettled that she had 'none of the evening leisure' that she'd promised herself. He gave up the other room, promising her faithfully that he would be able to work from home. His fidgety behaviour disturbed her and made her depressed. 'Of Charles ever bringing any work to pass at home, I am very doubtful,' she told Sarah.

But then, a new friend, the political writer William Godwin, came up with a specific project. He and his wife had gone into the children's publishing business, establishing their own company, the Juvenile Library. As a bachelor, Godwin had made just enough money for himself but now he was a husband and the father of a large family. The death of his first wife, Mary Wollstonecraft, in 1797, had left him with two daughters to bring up – their own, another Mary, and Fanny, Wollstonecraft's daughter by the American Gilbert Imlay. His second wife, Mary Jane Clairmont, whom he'd married in 1801, also had a daughter, confusingly called by the same name as her mother. The couple went on to have a son, another William, making them a family of two adults and four children and creating a pressing need for money.

Given such a household of children, it wasn't surprising that the Godwins turned their thoughts towards children's literature, particularly as they were both knowledgeable on the subject. Godwin's first wife, Wollstonecraft, had drawn on her experience as a governess and a schoolteacher to write *Original Stories from Real Life with Conversations Calculated to Regulate the Affections and Form the Mind to Truth and Goodness*, a book of such priggishness and cheerlessness it is hard to believe it was written by the young firebrand who wrote *A Vindication of the Rights of Woman*. The second Mrs Godwin had previously worked for the publisher Benjamin Tabart, editing his three-volume series of nursery stories and translating the fairytales of Charles Perrault.

And, in the early nineteenth century, children's literature was by no means a second-class form of writing. For some time, it had been shaping up into an interesting battleground of ideas for philosophers, churchmen, teachers and parents. Broadly speaking, the battle lines were drawn between the followers of people like Locke and Rousseau who believed a child can acquire wisdom and knowledge through experience and joyfully. For them, books needed to be entertaining, to feed the imagination and to encourage a sense of wonder. The Romantic poets – friends of the Lambs – ranged themselves on this side. In particular, Wordsworth's lyrical ballads speak eloquently of a child's capacity for wonder.

On the opposing side, there were the educationalists – people like Anna Barbauld and Sarah Trimmer – who inclined to the belief that children were full of original sin which had to be explained or drilled out of them. Sarah Trimmer, who was involved in the Sunday School movement, had a particular mistrust of fancy and poetical flights of the imagination. She went in for determinedly sprightly information, facts imparted in bite-size pieces with a little homily at the end. 'See those busy little ants,' she chirped in *An Easy Introduction to the Knowledge of Nature*, 'they are at work as hard as possible – Do you know that they get all the corn they can, and lay it up against the winter comes? – They bury their Dead – carry their young ones about, and do many laborious things – If all Men and women were as provident as they are, there would not be so many Beggars.' Anna Barbauld was a non-conformist and anti-slavery campaigner, a fundamentally decent woman who wrote dull books with titles like *Early Lessons for Children, Lessons for Children of Three Years Old* and *Lessons for Children*. By way of (limited) variety, she also wrote *Hymns in Prose for Children*. These books were literal, moralistic and probably more popular with parents than children. They introduced young readers to characters like Miss Ann Pearce who was 'such a good child that she would not have done a thing she was bid not to do for the world'. And her opposing number, Charlotte Philips, who disobeyed her mother's order not to play with candles, burnt herself and was scarred for life.

Sarah Trimmer was even more influential. Strong-minded and energetic, she founded and edited the periodical *The Guardian of Education*, the purpose of which was 'to contribute to the preservation of the young and innocent from the dangers which threaten them in the form of infantine and juvenile literature'. In the *Guardian*, she'd called Godwin's 1802 book, *Bible Stories, Memorable Acts of the Ancient Patriarchs, Judges and Kings*, 'an engine of mischief'. She mistrusted fairytales, believing

William Godwin by James Northcote.

that they frightened children as well as 'working too powerfully upon the feelings of the mind, or giving false pictures of life and manners'. Cinderella, she singled out for particular criticism because it encouraged a disturbing love of finery.

The debate between these two groups was intense and its implications profound. In asking what should a child read, they were also asking the question what is a child and, by extension, what is a human being.

Godwin was shrewd enough to recognise that it is parents

who buy books and that, in the marketplace at least, people like Sarah Trimmer had the upper hand. He knew that children's books could make money. John Newberry, whose name is commemorated in today's children's literature prize, had started his career as a bookseller in Reading and had built up a small fortune publishing books for children. His first, *A Little Pretty Pocket Book* was published in 1744 and cost 8d with a ball or pincushion or 6d without the covermount. Like many of the books he published, it also contained a plug for Dr James's Fever Powders, which were Newberry's sideline.

By the time Godwin entered the children's market, there were already plenty of books for children; the range was wide, from hymn books for youngsters to specially abridged editions of *Robinson Crusoe* and *Gulliver's Travels*. But there was no doubt which camp was holding sway. When Mary made a visit to Newberry's Shop, near St Paul's, to buy a book for Coleridge's young son, Derwent, she could find only the works of Barbauld and Trimmer, a fact which, when reported to Charles, resulted in him exploding with fury. He wrote angrily to Coleridge of 'Mrs B's and Mrs Trimmer's nonsense . . . Damn them, I mean the cursed Barbauld Crew, these Blights and Blasts of all that is Human in man and child.' He thought their stuff 'insignificant and vapid'.

Godwin, on the other hand, was probably more impressed by Mrs Barbauld when it came to setting up his business but then he was thinking of the practicalities and was aiming for a victory over his troublesome finances, not over children's hearts and minds, nor over moralising pedagogues. He once summed up his attitude to children's literature in a letter to Charles: '. . . it is children that read children's books, when they are read; but it is parents that choose them. The critical thought of the tradesman (publisher) puts itself therefore in the place of the parent, and what the parent will condemn.' His own reputation as a dangerous radical was a hindrance when it came to children's literature, so he used the name Thomas Hodgkins to take over the lease of a shop. The idea was to write children's books and sell them from there. If energy and determination were ever enough to succeed in business, he and his wife would have been a success. They were both hard-workers. Godwin took the pseudonyms Theophilus Marclife and Edward Baldwin and put them to work. Theophilus wrote *The Life Of Lady Jane Grey* and Edward was amazingly prolific, turning out *Fables Ancient and Modern* (an update of Aesop), *Pantheon* (a retelling of Greek legends), *History of England, History of Rome,* and *History of Greece.* Mrs Godwin too was busy; she produced *Dramas for Children* and *Rays of the Rainbow.*

They showed good judgement. One of their finds was *The Swiss Family Robinson* which was an enormous success and has been loved by generations of children. They hired William Blake to do illustrations for them and pressed all their friends to contribute. Hazlitt wrote a grammar for them and Charles Lamb turned in *The King and Queen of Hearts,* a jokey verse, extended out of the old nursery rhyme. Then, during the period when Mary and Charles were still in a 'fidget' about the farce, the Godwins came up with the idea for *Tales from Shakespeare.* The idea was probably based on *Contes moraux et instructifs à l'usage de la Jeunesse. Tirés des tragédies de Shakespeare,* which Mrs Godwin had translated. It retold the stories of Shakespeare, simplifying them for a young audience and ampli-fying their moral message. The plan, according to Mary, was to publish them as 'separate story books . . . single stories like the little shilling books'. Each book would retell a Shakespeare play for a young audience.

They probably asked just Charles to write it – his outburst against the 'cursed Barbauld crew' can be seen as him revving up his imagination by damning the competition – but he chose to delegate the bulk of the work to Mary and she took to it with gusto. It came at an ideal time, giving a much-needed jolt to her imagination and helping her shake off some of the miseries of the previous winter. Keen readers and playgoers, *Tales from Shakespeare* was an ideal project for them. Briskly and efficiently, they divided up the work, ignoring the history plays entirely, assigning the comedies to her and the tragedies to him. Perhaps they thought the tales of madness and murder in *King Lear, Hamlet* and *Othello* would be disturbing for her or they may have considered that the comedies with their romantic themes were more suitable for a woman to write. So Mary was confronted with fourteen complicated dramas, each of which included a large cast of characters acting out story-lines that were often both improbable and improper, written in styles that ranged from the poetic to the bawdy, the sublime to the ridiculous. To turn the plays into what were essentially short stories – the Godwins wanted each to be about 5,000 words – required firm editing and a keen judgement of narrative. Mary's handling of the material was both confident and skilled.

She did not re-write the plays; she did exactly what the title said, she wrote tales *from* Shakespeare, extracting from the poetry – to borrow Othello's phrase – 'a round unvarnished tale'. Essentially, she retold the plays as love stories, transforming Shakespeare's complex comedies into mini courtship novels. So in her version of *The Tempest*, she underplayed the themes of betrayal and reinstatement and concentrated on Miranda's new and wondering love for Ferdinand. In *A Midsummer's Night Dream*, she dropped Theseus and Hippolyta entirely, shrank the role of the fairy characters and built up the crossed-wires love affairs of the four mortals. There was none of Dogberry and his humour in Mary's *Much*

Ado About Nothing, only the romantic comedy of Benedick and Beatrice. And her *Two Gentlemen of Verona* features two pairs of idiots falling in and out of love without the knockabout fun of Launce and his dog. In *Tales from Shakespeare*, Mary was able to write about all the things she would never experience first-hand – love, marriage, marital happiness and marital disunity.

Shakespeare's verses, she wrote in the Preface, were the 'rich treasures', and hers were 'small and valueless coins', but none the less she was bold and imaginative in the changes she made. Where the blank verse worked for her – for example in song form – she quoted directly but, more usually, she took Shakespeare's poetry as a springboard for her own creativity. So Shakespeare's Puck is described as one who:

> ... frights the maidens of the villagery,
> Skim milk, and sometimes labour in the quern,
> And bootless make the breathless housewife churn.

Mary has her Puck: 'plunging his light and airy form in to the butter-churn, and while he was dancing his fantastic shape in the churn, in vain the dairymaid would labour to change her cream into butter'. The words are Mary's but, like all good adaptors, she honoured the spirit of the original.

She worked quickly. By the second week of May she had finished *The Tempest, A Winter's Tale, A Midsummer Night's Dream, Much Ado About Nothing, The Two Gentlemen of Verona* and *Cymbeline* and was hard at work on the *Merchant of Venice*. Charles had completed *Othello* and *Macbeth*. They shared the labour, often working alongside each other in the same room, pooling difficulties and suggesting solutions. According to Mary, the two of them sat: '... writing on one table (but not on one cushion sitting) like Hermia and Helena in the Midsummer's

Nights Dream, or rather like an old literary Darby and Joan, I taking snuff and he groaning all the while and saying he can make nothing of it, which he always says till he has finished and then he finds out he has made something of it.'

From the start, the joint project was more appealing to Mary and she made a better job of 'her' plays. The tragedies, his contribution to the *Tales*, were well done but his almost reverential love of Elizabethan language made them less direct and weaker as stories. Mary's comedies were highly skilled pieces of work, fresh and upbeat, with a distinct voice. Her own personality – judicious but kindly – was ever present. 'Maidens will do foolish things for love,' she wrote of Helena in *A Midsummer's Night's Dream* and she gets round some of the extravagances of character and plot with a cool line in understated irony. For example, of the law in Athens which condemns daughters to death if they refuse their father's choice of a husband, she writes: 'As fathers do not often desire the death of their own daughters, even though they do happen to prove a little refractory, this law was seldom or never put in execution, though perhaps the young ladies of that city were not unfrequently threatened by their parents with the terror of it.' No absurdity of plot could worry someone whose reading included some of the most lurid Gothic novels of the day.

Yet she also adopted, for the purpose of writing the *Tales*, a sophisticated manner, a worldly tone, reminiscent of Restoration comedy and which perhaps came out of her own unlived life, the one that emerged in her mania. Of Bassanio in *The Merchant of Venice*, she writes that he 'lived in too expensive a manner for his slender means, as young men of high rank with small fortunes are too apt to do'. And there is a knowing slyness about the line from *Twelfth Night* that 'servants soon discover when their ladies delight to converse with handsome young messengers'.

With plot difficulties that might have seemed indecent for young people, she simply changed them. For example, she made Marianna in *Measure for Measure* the wife of Angelo not his deserted mistress. Mary allowed herself a free hand with the material. At the time she was writing, Shakespeare was not yet the sanctified Bard he was to become. Just as he himself had borrowed, cribbed and adapted from earlier writers, it was the norm to take liberties with his plots. There was a popular version of *King Lear* by playwright Nahum Tate in which Lear and Cordelia survived. The actor/director David Garrick staged it this way and even wrote extra lines for Cordelia. Samuel Johnson liked it better than the original.

Mary had a keen sense of who she was writing for – a young girl, intelligent, keen to read but denied, because of her sex, access to books, a girl that could have been her younger self. 'For young ladies . . .' she wrote in the Preface, '. . . it has been the intention chiefly to write; because boys being generally permitted the use of their fathers' libraries at a much earlier age than girls are, they frequently have the best scenes of Shakespeare by ear, before their sisters are permitted to look into this manly book.' In *Tales from Shakespeare*, Mary feminises this 'manly book', bringing it into line with the sort of romantic fiction commonly directed at young girls.

Remembering perhaps how Charles had helped her, she called on boys to share their reading with their sisters: '. . . instead of recommending these Tales to the perusal of young gentlemen who can read them so much better in the originals, their kind assistance is rather requested in explaining to their sisters such parts as are hardest for them to understand.'

Halfway through writing the Preface, she ran out of steam and Charles took over, finishing up with a sentimental sop for the parents of their potential readers, a wish – worthy of Mrs Barbauld, that: 'the true Plays of Shakespeare may prove to them in older years – enrichers of the fancy, strengtheners of virtue, a withdrawing form all selfish and mercenary thoughts, a lesson of all sweet and honourable thoughts and actions, to teach courtesy, benignity, generosity, humanity: for of examples, teaching these virtues, his pages are full'.

Mary relied on Charles to correct her spelling and grammar and he encouraged her when she ran into difficulties. 'She complains of having to set forth so many female characters in boy's clothes,' he wrote to Wordsworth. 'She begins to think Shakespeare must have wanted imagination, – I to encourage her, for she often faints in the prosecution of her great work, flatter her with telling her of how well such a play and such a play is done. But she is stuck fast and I have been obliged to promise to assist her.' But really he was impressed; she did the plays 'capitally', he said.

Their attitude to their work was very different. Charles, at this point in his life, wanted to be a playwright. He saw the *Tales* as jobbing hack work. 'I think it will be popular among the little people,' he wrote rather dismissively. Mary, on the other hand, was experiencing all the pleasure of the first time writer. In between cooking shoulders of lamb, she puzzled over narrative problems. She was proud to have 'work' to talk of. When she wrote to Sarah about her *Tales*, she bubbled over with energy and enthusiasm. 'My tales seem to be all the subject matter I write about,' she apologised. She was enjoying that boost of confidence, that sense of all things being possible which comes with completed work. 'I go on very well and have no doubt but I shall always be able to hit upon some such kind of job to keep going on,' she declared confidently. The idea of earning money of her own doing work she enjoyed gave her an enormous thrill; 'I think I shall get fifty pounds a year at the lowest calculation,' she speculated. 'But as I have not yet seen any money of my own earning for we do not expect to be paid till Christmas I do not feel the good fortune that has so unexpectedly befallen me half so much as I ought to do.'

In late June, Charles's farce, *Mr H*, was accepted and Mary was delighted but cautious. 'You must come and see it the first night,' she wrote to Sarah. 'For if it succeeds it will be a great pleasure to you, and if it should not we shall want your consolation.' Yet it was still the *Tales* that really absorbed her. She became badly blocked with *All's Well That Ends Well*. It 'teased' her 'more than all the rest put together', she complained to Sarah. Having 'picked out the best stories first these latter ones take more time being more perplext and unmanageable. They sometimes plague me as bad as your Lovers do you.' The play's plot follows the fortunes of a young woman, Helena, the impoverished daughter of a skilled physician. She has fallen in love with Bertram, the son of her friend and patron, the Countess of Rousillon. In a neat reversal of the usual fairytale hero wins fair maiden quest, Helena is promised a husband if she can cure the king of France of an illness that has baffled his doctors. She succeeds, using one of her father's special potions, and claims Bertram as her husband. He rejects her, abandoning her with the words: 'When thou canst get the ring upon my finger which never shall come off, and show me a child begotten of they body that I am father to, then call me husband; but to such a "then" I write a "never".' On receiving the false news of her death, he sets out to seduce Diana. Helena befriends Diana, swaps places with her and entertains Bertram at midnight, swapping her 'honour' for the ring on his finger. Once Bertram is confronted with the truth of the bed trick and shown the ring, he capitulates and promises to love Helena, 'dearly, ever ever dearly'. The play's plot is far-fetched, the bed trick unsuitable for young people, and it was hard to find an obvious moral in this tale of female determination and male unkindness. In the end, Mary dealt with it by turning the bed trick into a 'night's interview', a meeting of two minds in which Helena 'exerted all her wit to please him; and the simple graces of her lively conversation and the endearing sweetness of her manners so charmed Bertram, that he vowed she should be his wife'.

While writing, Mary even lost interest in Sarah Stoddart's love affairs. She made the usual enquiries but her mind was elsewhere. 'You must not mind the many wretchedly dull letters I have sent you for indeed I cannot help, my mind is so dry after poring over my work all day,' she told her friend. But the letters were not dry, they were overflowing with excitement and energy. She gave all her mind and time to her work, turning down a holiday invitation from Sarah. 'We thought if we went anywhere and left them undone, they would lay upon our minds; and that when we returned, we should feel unsettled.' Even before she has quite finished the *Tales*, her mind is turning on other projects. 'I shall soon have done my work,' she wrote, 'and know not what to begin next. Now will you set your brains to work and invent a story either for a short child's story or a long one that would make a kind of Novel or a Story that would make a play. Charles wants me to write a play but I am not over anxious to set about it, but seriously will you draw me out a skeleton of a story either from memory of any thing that you have read or from your own invention and I will fill it up in some way or other.'

Once she'd finished, she thought constantly about more writing. 'I have been busy making waistcoats and plotting new work to succeed the Tales,' she reported on 23 October, 'as yet I have not hit upon any thing to my mind.' By early December, she was embarked on a new work, but its progress was a quiet affair compared with the excitement generated by *Mr H*. After being on the backburner for months, it finally had its opening night set – 10 December. It was given an eye-catching playbill; an enormous letter H was splashed across it and Charles was full of hopes. He wrote: 'I shall get £200 from the theatre if Mr. H. has a good run & I hope £100 for the copyright. Nothing if it fails; & there never was a more ticklish thing. The whole depends on the manner in which the name is brought out, which I value myself on, a Chef d'œuvre.'

It was the day of the play's opening night and Mary and Charles's friends were eager and supportive. Hazlitt wrote: 'Bright shone the morning on the play – bills that announced thy appearance and the streets were filled with the buzz of person asking one another if they would go to see Mr H – and answering that they would certainly.' Mary and Charles took a party of friends to the theatre. There was Hazlitt and Henry Crabb Robinson and John Lamb brought a large group of his colleagues from the East India House. They sat in the pit near the orchestra and waited for the audience reaction. The prologue went down well but then the play proper opened and with it came a long sibilant stream of hisses. The play on which Charles had lavished more than a year of his free time and so much of his energy was an embarrassing failure. Henry Crabb Robinson complained loyally of the 'vulgar taste' of the pit in hissing but 'damned' was the word used by the clear-sighted and more frankly spoken Hazlitt. Charles put a brave face on it, even joining in with the hisses but the experience was obviously devastating. To Wordsworth, he explained the flop by saying 'the subject was not substantial enough'. The truth would have been harder to face; in Mr H, Charles had written a farce that wasn't very funny. The play's story was about a vain young man who appears in Bath and intrigues everyone by his mysterious name – Mr H. When his full moniker is finally revealed, it turns out to be Hogsflesh. No wonder the sophisticated metropolitan audience hissed.

Mary was devastated by the play's reception, so upset that Charles feared she would go out of her mind. He refused to let her write to anyone; it was he who told Sarah Stoddart of the play's failure, explaining that 'Mary is by no means unwell but I made her let me write.' Later in the month, when the danger of her falling ill had passed for the moment, Mary admitted to another friend: 'I tried the morning after the failure of our little farce to write a line to let you know its ill success, and how stoutly we meant to bear it, but I found myself utterly incapable of writing one connected sentence.'

Despite her distress, Mary could be analytical about Charles's writing. 'The blame rested chiefly with Charles and yet should not be called blame for it was mere ignorance of stage effect – and, I am mistaken if he has not gained much useful knowledge, more than he could have learned from a constant attendance on the representation of other people's pieces, by seeing his own fail, he seems perfectly aware why, & from what cause it failed. He intends to write one more, with all his dear bought experience in his head, and should that share the same fate, he will then turn his mind to some other pursuit.'

The following month, with considerably less fanfare, *Tales from Shakespeare* came out in two volumes. Mary was given no credit; Charles didn't want any and was cross that his name was on the book. He also complained about the production; he particularly hated the plates that had been chosen by 'the bad baby' – Charles's nickname for Mrs Godwin. He sent a copy of *Tales* to William Wordsworth, with a lightly dismissive appraisal: 'We think *Pericles* of hers the best, and *Othello* of mine – but I hope all have some good. *As You Like It* we like least.'

The critics were kinder. In their view, *Tales from Shakespeare* was a success. The *Critical Review* said: 'We have compared it with many of the numerous systems which have been devised for riveting attention at an early age, and insinuating knowledge subtly and pleasantly into minds, by nature averse from it. The result of the comparison is not so much that it rises high in the list, as that it claims the very first place, and stands unique, and without rival or competitor.'

The first edition sold out on the first day. The Godwins kept a close eye on who was reading it. An advertisement in the second edition of 1809 explained that: 'It has been the general sentiment, that the style in which these Tales are written, is not so precisely adapted for the amusement of mere children, as for an acceptable and improving present to young ladies advancing to the state of womanhood.' Since then, it has never been out of print. Godwin's other winner, *The Swiss Family Robinson*, is the only other children's book from the early nineteenth century that is still being read today.

And although Mary's name didn't appear on the book, it was well known among her circle of friends that she had written most of it. The success of *Tales* gave her pleasure and confidence in her writing ability. However, before she could get to work on anything else, she became ill again.

Her relapse took place while she and her brother were on holiday in Suffolk. They were guests of the Clarksons, anti-slavery agitators and good friends of the Wordsworths. All had been going well; Mary and the Clarksons' son had raided a cherry tree together and there had been pleasant visits to neighbours and gossip about mutual friends. Then, in an extravagant gesture, Mary gave away one of Charles's coats to the Clarksons' servant – impetuous gestures of largesse are typical at the start of mania – and it became clear that she was falling ill. Charles moved quickly to get her back to London and into an asylum. They took leave of the Clarksons in such a hurry that she left all their manuscripts and books behind. The journey back to London began reasonably well.

Mary was, according to Charles, 'tolerably quiet'. Soon though she was 'very bad indeed' and Charles had to call on other friends of the Clarksons, the Knights who lived in Essex, just on the outskirts of London. They provided Mary with a strait-jacket and, with her arms confined, she and Charles continued their difficult coach journey. Mary 'talked in the most wretched desponding way conceivable', said Charles and by the time they reached the asylum at Hoxton she was 'sadly tired and miserably depressed'.

Her illness lasted for about two months and the memory of having been so ill and so publicly remained with her as a source of pain. She confided her unhappiness to Dorothy Wordsworth, writing 'feelingly of the distress she had given' the Clarksons. The episode had also damped 'her own hopes of going from home again to any friend's house'. She needed time to regain her confidence to go travelling again but she suffered no anxieties regarding her writing. When Godwin asked her to come up with an idea of her own, she was more than ready.

FRONTISPIECE

In this manner, the epitaph on my mother's tomb being my primer and my spelling-book, I learned to read. —— Page 9.

MRS. LEICESTER'S SCHOOL:

OR,

THE HISTORY

OF

SEVERAL YOUNG LADIES,

RELATED BY THEMSELVES.

London:

PRINTED FOR M. J. GODWIN, AT THE JUVENILE

LIBRARY, NO. 41, SKINNER-STREET.

1809.

Chapter 9

Mothers and Daughters

From the time of her death no one had ever spoken
to me of my mother, and I had apparently forgotten
her
      Mary Lamb, 'The Father's Wedding Day',
      Mrs Leicester's School, 1808

FOR HER NEXT PROJECT, Mary was inspired by a form of narrative older than Shakespeare, as old perhaps as storytelling itself; she brought together a group of young girls, all strangers to each other, and had each of them tell a story to the others. Mary was not the first to adapt *The Canterbury Tales'* format to juvenile literature. When she sat down to write *Mrs Leicester's School*, she was working within a genre that was already well established. The first of its kind had appeared more than fifty years earlier with the publication of *The Governess; or, Little Female Academy*, the work of Sarah Fielding, sister to the novelist Henry. Sarah wrote and Henry handled all her dealings with publishers; between them, with *The Governess*, they scored a notable success. *Mrs Leicester's School* was just one of the forty or so imitators it inspired in the eighteenth and nineteenth centuries. But Mary took liberties with the format and made it very much her own.

The Governess, as its title suggested, had a frankly moral purpose. Its dedication – to a Mrs Poyntz – declared the book to be an attempt to: 'cultivate an early inclination to Benevolence, and a Love of Virtue, in the minds of young women, by trying to shew them that their true interest is concerned in cherishing and improving those amiable Dispositions into Habits; and in keeping down all rough and boisterous Passions; and that from this alone they can propose to themselves to arrive at true Happiness, in any of the Stations of Life allotted to the female character.' The Preface developed this theme. 'The Design of the following sheets is to prove to you, that Pride, Stubbornness, Malice, Envy, and, in short, all manner of wickedness, is the greatest Folly we can be persuaded of, and constantly turns on the Head of that foolish person who does not conquer and get the better of all Inclinations to such Wickedness.' In contrast, *Mrs Leicester's School* kept preaching to a minimum.

Mrs Teachum, the governess of the little female academy, was a strict disciplinarian. A clergyman's widow, she 'never omitted reprehending, and that pretty severely, any girl that was guilty of the smallest Fault proceeding from an Evil Disposition'. In *Mrs Leicester's School*, Mary created a kind teacher, one who empathises with her new pupils: 'The traces of tears were on every cheek, and I also was sad; for I, like you, had parted from my friends.' She also downplayed her role as moraliser. Mary's nameless teacher was no fount of wisdom and teaching; instead she declared herself to be only the 'amanuensis' – merely a literary assistant who has listened to the stories and is hoping 'to have a fair copy ready to present to each of you of your own biographical conversations last winter'. She hoped that she'd executed the office 'with a tolerably faithful pen'.

In *The Governess*, a quarrel over an apple leads these young goddesses – they have names like Lucy Sly and Dolly Friendly and Henny Fret – into a catfight that leaves them with torn hair and ripped clothes. On Mrs Teachum's return, they start blaming each other. They are calmed down by their teacher and led into a series of storytelling by the eldest girl, an appalling little prig called Jenny Peace. The children's autobiographies are straightforward lessons about misbehaviour, punishment and improvement; for example, Dolly Friendly confesses how she lied for her sister's sake. They also tell fairy stories such as the fanciful tale of the cruel Giant Barbarico, the good Giant Ebenefico and the pretty little Edward Mignon. But Mrs Teachum greeted the flights of fancy with limited enthusiasm. Giants were magic and magic was all very well but too far removed from the simplicity of taste and manner that Mrs Teachum was after. Imitators of *The Governess*, which included Mary Wollstonecraft's *Original Stories From Real Life* (1788), written when she was a nursery governess in Ireland, and Maria Edgeworth's *The Parent's Assistant* (1796), used this combination of Scheherazade and the confessional. Mary, however, chose to drop the fairytales and made the girls' own stories the central interest. In doing so, she moved the school story format into a new, much more interesting psychological territory.

It was virgin territory. Mrs Leicester's school was brand new, the pupils were all new, away from home for the first time. According to the teacher, 'this was very unlike the entrance to an old established school, where there is always some good natured girl who will shew attention to a new scholar, and take pleasure in initiating her into the customs and amusements of the place. These, thought I, have their own amusements to invent; their own customs to establish.' The girls are a space waiting to be written in, fictional forms of Locke's *tabula rasa*.

Gradually, the teacher drew them in. 'I invited you to draw near a bright fire which blazed in the chimney, and looked the only cheerful thing in the room. During our first solemn silence, which, you may remember was only broken by my repeated requests that you would make a smaller, and still smaller circle, till I saw the fireplace was fairly inclosed round.' Once they were seated round the fire – the campfire? – the teacher issued a general invitation to confide. '"Begin,"' said I, "with your name . . . Tell us the first thing you can remember; relate whatever happened to make a great impression on you when you were very young, and if you find you can connect your story till your arrival here to-day, I am sure we shall listen to you with pleasure."'

Elizabeth Villiers tells the first story, entitled 'The Sailor Uncle'. The first two sentences are unexceptional: 'My father is the curate of a village church, about five miles from Amwell. I was born in the parsonage-house, which joins the church-yard.' Then comes the shocker: 'The first thing I can remember was my father teaching me the alphabet from the letters on a tombstone that stood at the head of my mother's grave.' Here was Mary, a woman who had committed matricide, and the minute she was given the opportunity to choose her own subject matter, she plunged immediately into a story about the death of a young girl's mother.

Elizabeth Villiers has not mourned her mother because no one has told her that her death is a sorrowful matter. Her father says: 'Go and see pretty mamma. Go and learn pretty letters.' And the girl does: 'the epitaph on my mother's tomb being my primer and my spelling book'. It is as if the 'words on the tombstone were somehow a part of mamma'. As literacy brings the engraved symbols into meaning for Elizabeth, so her mother remains a living presence. 'All was cheerfulness and good humour in our visits to mamma, as we called it. My father would tell me how quietly mamma slept there, and that he and his little Betsy would one day sleep beside mamma in that grave.'

The arrival of her mother's brother – the sailor uncle of the title – jolts her into knowledge. She witnesses his grief and begins to feel her own. 'Now I first learned that my mother's death was a heavy affliction; for I heard my father tell a melancholy story of her long illness, her death, and what he had suffered from her loss.' Just as Mary had emerged from her first fit of violent mania to discover what she had done, Elizabeth is forced out of her unknowing state into a realisation of the profound implications of her mother's death. 'From that time,' she says, 'I never ceased pondering on the sad story of my dead mamma.'

Keen to wean the child away from the graveyard, the uncle undertakes to teach her to read using books instead of tomb lettering. 'I could now read very well, and the continual habit of listening to the conversation of my father and my uncle made me a little woman in understanding.' The story is about growth to maturity through language and the acquisition of knowledge through suffering. Her uncle teaches her about her mother until she comes to understand that she was a 'real mamma' not, as she had imagined, 'an ideal something, noway connected with life'. Elizabeth Villiers learns how to grieve and how to understand and comfort other people's grief. When her uncle leaves, she experiences it as a second loss, its poignancy sharpened by the fact that she had been angry with this kind man when he first arrived. This time, her father helps her through this grieving process, telling her: 'let it be a lesson to you to be as kind as possible to those you love; and remember, when they are gone from you, you will never think you had been kind enough. Such feelings as you have now described are the lot of humanity. So you will feel when I am no more;

and so will your children feel when you are dead.'

Elizabeth Villiers's tale encapsulates the theme of the whole collection. Out of the seven stories written by Mary – the other three were by Charles – five are centred round painful family dynamics. The three best – 'The Sailor Uncle', 'The Changeling' and 'The Father's Wedding Day' – are explicitly about mothers and daughters. Mary wanted to talk about her mother – the mother who, as she had written to Sarah Stoddart, was in her heart night and day – but this was more than a hundred years before the talking cure; the people who loved Mary tried to keep her mind away from painful subjects. According to Talfourd, Charles 'was always afraid of her sensibilities being too deeply engaged, and if in her presence any painful accident or history was discussed, he would turn the conversation with some desperate joke'. Another of their friends, Matilda Betham, recalled how he interrupted what he thought was a too intense conversation between herself and Mary Lamb with the words: 'Come, come, we must not talk sentimentally,' and turned the conversation on to lighter subjects. It was only in her writing that Mary was free from censorship, and the pages of *Mrs Leicester's School* became a record of her heart and soul. There, she was able to talk about mothers and daughters and the complex, painful feelings such thoughts raised in her. In this, her last book of prose, she worked out the great theme of her life – the loss of maternal love, the death of the mother and their corollary, the hauntingly difficult journey of grief.

Ann Withers, the narrator of 'The Changeling', has been robbed twice of a mother's love. Shortly after her birth, her mother is employed to act as a wet nurse to the baby daughter of Sir Edward and Lady Harriot Lesley. In this story, we have two mothers who are unable to care for their own children. The rich mother can't because she has a fever; the poor mother can't because she has to breastfeed the rich woman's child.

Harsh economics have driven a wedge between mother and child. The poor mother 'looked on me, and then on the little lady-baby, and she wept over me to think she was obliged to leave me to the charge of a careless girl, debarred from my own natural food, while she was nursing another person's child'. So she swaps the two children over and the switch, once made, remains in place long after the babies are weaned.

The nurse's daughter is brought up as a fine lady and Lady Harriot's daughter grows up in the nurse's cottage. The two girls become friends and are allowed to learn their lessons together until, one day, the changeling child learns the secret and decides to expose it to everybody around her. Her motive is altruistic, she feels her friend has been hard done by – 'something must be done, I thought, to make her amends for the injury she had sustained' – and cannot anticipate how the revelation might affect her. So she writes a play in which the baby swap is enacted – Mary had read her *Hamlet* well – and it is staged in front of her assumed parents and her real mother. The result is the wet nurse becomes hysterical and confesses. Despite the tears, despite the shock, the roles are briskly reversed and Lady Harriot's biological daughter is taken back into the grand house and back into her mother's love. Like Mary, the young Ann had been the 'unconscious instrument' of her own disaster. Her mother welcomes her real daughter back with remarkable ease, loves her instantly and swiftly drops the other assumed daughter. This seemingly effortless replacement is complete, marked by a shared talent for music from which the non-biological daughter is excluded. 'Here she was her mother's own girl indeed,' mourns the unhappy, dispossessed girl. The reunited mother and daughter play together in harmony as poor Ann Withers looks on: 'Nothing makes the heart ache with such a hopeless, heavy pain, as envy . . . All the day long the notes of the harp or the piano spoke sad sounds to me, of the loss of a loved mother's heart.'

Ann is not even returned to her natural mother – the nurse, sick with shame and repentance, is taken away to look after someone else's family. Instead, Ann continues to live on in Lady Harriot's house, displaced and unhappy, demoted from her social position and essentially abandoned by her parents. 'Formerly when speaking of them, I used, proud of their titles, to delight to say, "Sir Edward or Lady Harriot did this, or this," now I would give worlds to say, "My father or my mother."' Lady Harriot admits that she is now so fond of her restored daughter that she has forgotten her 'solemn promise . . . never to forget how long she had loved me as her child'.

So poor Ann is sent away to school, a decision that comes as a relief to everyone, herself included. 'I endeavoured to submit to my hard fate with cheerfulness, and prepared myself, not without reluctance, to quit a mansion which had been scene of so many enjoyments, and latterly of such very different feelings.' 'The Changeling' is a cruel story in which children are discarded and acquired with a terrible casualness.

The heroine of 'The Father's Wedding Day' has also been sent to school after being displaced by another child. Here Elinor Forester loses her mother at a very early age but shortly afterwards gains a stepmother. 'My father sat me on his knee, and as he often used to do after the death of my mother, he called me his dear little orphaned Elinor, and then he asked me if I loved Miss Saville. I replied "yes". Then he said this dear lady was going to be so kind as to be married to him, and that she was to be my mamma.' Elinor misunderstands him and is delighted to think that Miss Saville is going to be literally transformed into her dead mother. The reality – a living breathing stepmother whose black eyes and red cheeks are the very opposite of her own pale and delicate mother – horrifies her and she rejects her.

Everyone but the former Miss Saville is angry with her. It is the new stepmother who talks Elinor through her memory of her mother, who takes her through grief to healing. 'I pointed out to her all the things that I remembered to have belonged to mamma, and she encouraged me to tell her all the little incidents which had dwelt on my memory concerning her. She told me, that she went to school with mamma when she was a little girl and that I should come into this room with her every day when papa was gone out, and she would tell me stories of mamma when she was a little girl no bigger than me.'

The new stepmother helps the child understand her loss, she gives her space to talk about her mother, she adds to the girl's store of knowledge about her mother. She plays the same role to Elinor as the sailor uncle does to Elizabeth Villiers – she brings the little girl to an understanding that death is final and that memories of the dead person must be treasured. By talking of the dead person – something Mary Lamb was unable to do – there comes emotional maturity and a measure of peace. However, when the stepmother has a child of her own, Elinor is sent away. 'She has been my only instructress...' she says. 'She would have continued to teach me, but she has not time, for she has a little baby of her own now, and that is the reason I came to school.'

Tales from Shakespeare was the story of love triumphant, a festival of young and unlikely love winning against the odds. *Mrs Leicester's School* was an elegy for love gone wrong. Again and again, maternal love is withheld, sought for, lost, regained and then lost again. We meet girls dealing with grief, growing through pain, learning through experience. Three years before writing *Mrs Leicester's School*, Mary had written to comfort Dorothy Wordsworth over the death of her brother at sea. 'I wished to tell you, that you would one day feel the kind of peaceful state of mind, and sweet memory of the dead which you so happily describe as now almost begun, but I felt that it was improper, and most grating to the feelings of the afflicted, to say to them that the memory of their affliction would in time become a constant part not only of their "dream, but of their most wakeful sense of happiness". That you would see every object with, and through your lost brother, and that that would at least become a real and everlasting source of comfort to you, I felt, and well know from my own experience in sorrow, but till you yourself began to feel this I did not dare tell you so.' *Mrs Leicester's School* showed that process in action – that move from 'sorrow' to a 'peaceful state of mind'. This time, Mary put her mark on the book, albeit obliquely: the dedication is signed MB – the first and last letters of her name.

The book struck an instant chord with its readers. The *Critical Review* had only 'unqualified praise' for its 'delightfully simple and exquisitely told' stories; the diarist and literary commentator Henry Crabb Robinson thought 'The Changeling' was 'an admirable tale, full of deep feeling and great truth of imagination' and that the whole collection exhibited 'grace and talent'. It was reprinted four times in six years. More than that, it *touched* its readers. The poet Walter Landor thought that 'The Father's Wedding Day' was 'with the sole exception of the "Bride of Lammermoor"! . . . the most beautiful tale in prose composition in any language, ancient or modern'. He was deeply moved by it, struck by the young girl's confusion, the way she wants to show her mother her clothes but, of course, she can't because the only reason she is in wedding finery is because her mother is dead. 'How natural, how novel is all this!' thought Landor. 'Did you ever imagine that a fresh source of the pathetic would burst forth before us in this trodden and hardened world. I never did, and when I found myself upon it, I pressed my temples with both hands, and tears ran down to my elbows.' Coleridge made a margin note on his copy of Mrs Leicester's School: 'It at once soothes and amuses me to think – nay to know – that the time will come when this little volume of my dear and well-nigh eldest friend, dear Mary Lamb, will be not only enjoyed but acknowledged as a rich jewel in the treasury of our permanent English literature.'

Mrs Leicester's School was published at the end of 1808. By April of the following year, Mary and Charles were again at work together, on the collection of verse that was published as Poetry for Children that summer. It was subtitled 'entirely original, by the Author of Mrs Leicester's School' and most of the verses were Mary's. Charles declared his contribution to be 'but one third in quantity of the whole'. Her elder brother John also contributed; his poem 'The Beggar Man' is a tiny elegy for the destitute man, the general neglect as contrasted with his parents' former love and attention.

Once a mother's tender care.
When too young to understand
He but scorch'd his little hand,
By the candle's flaming light
Attracted, dancing, spiral, bright,
Clasping fond her darling round,
A thousand kisses heal'd the wound,
Now abject, stooping, old, and wan,
No mother tends the beggar-man.

John Lamb had a ready sympathy for the underdog and could find that beast in unlikely places. He wrote an impassioned pamphlet against cruelty to animals which included an attack on the habit of boiling eels alive. He entered wholeheartedly and somewhat surreally into the fish's feelings. 'If an eel had the wisdom of Solomon, he could not help himself in the ill-usage that befalls him; but if he had, and were told, that it was necessary for our subsistence that he should be eaten, that he must be skinned first, and then broiled; if ignorant of man's usual practice, he could conclude that the cook would so far use her reason as to cut off his head first, which is not fit for food, as then he might be skinned and broiled without harm.' He nagged Charles to get it published for him and Charles did his best, sending it to Henry Crabb Robinson but he saw the ludicrousness of the project because he begged his friend not to show it to a mutual female friend because 'she makes excellent Eel soup and the leading points of the book are directed against that very process'. John Lamb attacked the Corn Laws as being detrimental to the poor and defended the practice of gleaning whereby the poor could gather the bits of grain that were left behind in the field after harvest. Gleaning, he wrote, was 'the nicest word in the language . . . it pictured man satisfied with having secured himself from want, looking on pleased that his less fortunate fellow-creatures, who, like the fowls of the air, gather not into barns, should have a taste of the bounty of Heaven at this holiday time of the year'.

John had clearly got over his terror at the prospect of Mary not being permanently confined; he was a frequent visitor at his brother and sister's apartment and his siblings were on courteous terms with his wife. But the Lambs' friends disliked him. Proctor said he was 'generally abrupt and unprepossessing in manner . . . assuredly deficient in that courtesy which usually springs from a mind at friendship with the world'. Talfourd said he was 'so grossly rude and vulgarly so'.

Poetry for Children signalled an end for Charles; the poems themselves, as Charles so accurately judged, were 'but humble'. Some have charm and Charles was especially proud of 'the number of subjects, all of children, pick'd out by an old Bachelor and an old Maid. Many Parents would not have found so many.' But he also felt that he and Mary were pretty much 'worked out of child's work'.

There was no need, though, for them to stop writing altogether. At this point, Mary was in a strong position; any publisher might have been glad to use her. She had written two skilled, inventive and well-received books for girls. She had proved herself to be a fast, efficient writer to order as well as an imaginative creator of characters and situations. Mary, in the summer of 1809, could easily have expected to go on writing but, apart from some poems – written for private consumption – and a fascinating essay, her work all but dried up. After just two years and two books, her writing, as a career, was basically over. Years later, she told Henry Crabb Robinson that writing, for her, had been 'a most painful occupation, which only necessity could make her attempt'. This though was a kind of revisionism; she missed her writing. It had excited and energised her. It was her health that undermined her writing.

In the two years following the publication of *Poetry for Children*, she was very ill indeed. She had a severe attack of madness in the summer of 1809. Their landlord at Mitre Court reclaimed their rooms – 'their dear old dirty chambers' Mary called them – and she and her brother had an unsettled spring, moving temporarily to Southampton Buildings before settling in Inner Temple Lane. It was close to their birthplace and their new home – 'two rooms on third floor and five rooms above, with an inner staircase ... and all new painted ... for £30 a year' – ran Charles's description – was an improvement on the old but the move disturbed Mary, causing her 'great labour, and pain and grief'. She felt 'quite unsettled and un-homed'. She couldn't sleep properly in the new place and following on from her insomnia came an attack of her madness. She was ill that autumn until a visit to the Hazlitts in Winterslow restored her spirits. In March of the following year, she wrote that she was working again – 'I have been striving very hard to get through with something before you come' – she confided to Sarah but whatever it was it never came to fruition. In August she was ill again and, in November she experienced an attack of such severity that even Charles was terrified. Her medical adviser, Dr Tuthill, told her to drink only water and she claimed the new regime agreed with her. Charles attempted to follow suit but unsuccessfully and, after a while, Mary admitted that water drinking was 'very flat'. Such plain living was never likely to suit a woman who enjoyed a stiff brandy. Another of her pleasures – visits from Sarah Stoddart Hazlitt – were given up; Charles insisted, writing to Hazlitt, 'I have made up my mind that she shall never have any one in the house again with her, and that no one shall sleep with her not even for a night, for it is a very serious thing to be always living with a kind of fever upon her, and therefore I am sure you will take it in good part if I say that if Mrs Hazlitt comes to town at any time, however glad we shall be to see her in the daytime, I cannot ask her to spend a night under our roof.' He tried to keep friends away, asking the Godwins not to call in the mornings. It was necessary, he insisted, if they were to have 'tranquillity at home'. Mary, he said, was torn between causing offence 'and the difficulty of maintaining a system which she feels we must do to live without wretchedness'.

These bouts of illness left her depressed; she thought with regret of the writing she couldn't do. 'It is a great mortification to me to be such a useless creature,' she wrote mournfully to Dorothy Wordsworth. 'I am doing nothing,' she complained. 'I wish I was, for if I were once more busily employed at work, I should be more satisfied with myself. I should not feel so helpless and so useless.' Writing had empowered her; it was one of her life's sorrows that she was unable to go on with it.

She was irritated by domestic troubles. A newly engaged maid promptly fell ill and took to her bed, turning out to be yet another woman who had worn herself out by looking after an ailing mother. Shortly afterwards – possibly as a consequence – Mary herself was ill again.

Perhaps if they'd desperately needed the money, she might have gone on writing. And if Charles had continued his professional relationship with Godwin, more work might have come her way. But the Lambs' need for money was less pressing as Charles's salary from the East India House had been increased by £20 a year. He was turning his attention to journalism and, throughout 1809 and 1810, he began to write for Leigh Hunt's *The Reflector*, contributing articles on Hogarth and Shakespeare. Also, he didn't really see eye to eye with Godwin on what was suitable material for young children; they'd argued over Charles's *Adventures of Ulysses* which Godwin wanted to see toned down.

Mary continued to write – in particular she wrote poetry when she felt moved – but, on the brink of what could have become a very interesting body of work, she gave up writing professionally. She did not, however, give up writers. At one time, Charles had thought that Mary's illness and Mary's crime made them marked and cursed and outcast; the truth was they were incredibly popular. They couldn't have hidden even if they'd wanted to. People sought them out and the two of them became noted, remembered and recorded for the parties they threw.

Sir Thomas Talfourd
by John Lucas.

William Wordsworth
by Richard Carruthers.

James Leigh Hunt
by Margaret Gillies.

Henry Crabb Robinson
by Henry Darvall.

Chapter 10

Wit and Good Fellowship

... men of boisterous spirits, sitters up a-nights, disputants, drunken, yet seemed to have something noble about them. We dealt about this wit, or what passed for it after midnight, jovially.
        'Confessions of a Drunkard',
        Charles Lamb, 1833

The conversation of authors is not so good as might be imagined; but, such as it is (and with rare exceptions) it is better than any other.
        'On the Conversation of Authors',
        William Hazlitt, 1820

'SWIPES EXACTLY AT NINE, punch to commence at ten, with argument; difference of opinion expected to take place about eleven; perfect unanimity with some haziness and dimness before twelve.' That, according to Charles, was the essence of the Lambs' weekly parties. A group of like-minded people casually dropping by once a week was formalised into what Lamb jokingly called his 'public day'.

These evenings were not elaborate nor glittering, they were pure Bohemia, the best place in the world for people who are in flight from their pasts as the Lambs were. Regular but informal, relaxed in terms of dress and behaviour, they were highly charged with debate and often argument. They mixed writers, actors, lawyers, the famous and the unknown. William Wordsworth came when he was in town and so too did Mrs Reynolds, an elderly lady who used to live in the Inner Temple and who had once taught Charles. The guests were, according to one of Charles's friends and biographers, 'persons of an uncertain fortune . . . in the world's eye, a ragged regiment'.

Most of them were struggling financially, living in cramped lodgings and boarding houses, but their minds were expansive, full of dreams of revolution and poetry. Many were brilliant, still more were unsteady, some were almost unhinged. For the best part of a decade, Mary and Charles entertained this distinctive group of people; the evenings were put off only when she was ill. Without her presence Charles was too depressed to have visitors.

Between them, Mary and Charles created something special: evenings that were buzzy with excitement and intellectual activity. Their weekly at-homes became happenings, events that lingered in people's minds and were immortalised in print. Mary's personality – gossipy, interested in others, non-judgmental – was key to the success of these parties. The once undereducated, undervalued drudge found herself presiding over a court of wits, writers, thinkers and radicals.

The surroundings were unglamorous. Number 4 Inner Temple Lane, to which the Lambs moved in the spring of 1809, was bigger and more comfortable than Mitre Court Buildings but their friends had to scramble up several flights of stairs to see them and the rooms themselves, though welcoming, were shabby. Talfourd recalled the apartment affectionately. 'The furniture is old-fashioned and worn: the ceiling low, and not wholly unstained by traces of the "great plant", though now virtuously forborne: but the Hogarths, in narrow black frames, abounding in infinite thought, humour and pathos, enrich the walls: and all things wear an air of comfort and hearty English welcome.' Henry Crabb Robinson noticed the books, 'the finest collection of shabby books I ever saw; such a number of first-rate works in very bad condition is, I think, nowhere to be found'. And in Hazlitt's words, 'Wit and good fellowship was the motto inscribed over the door.'

It was the people who made these evenings special. Crabb Robinson said he 'spent many happy hours' at the Lambs' and 'there saw a greater number of excellent persons than I had ever seen collected in one apartment'. The philosophers Godwin and Hazlitt came; Godwin to play cards and discuss social reform, Hazlitt to praise and defend Napoleon. Then there was Captain James Burney, the brother of the best-selling novelist Fanny Burney. The captain had sailed with Captain Cook on his second and third voyages and was busy writing what was to become the five-volume *A Chronological History of the Voyages and Discoveries in the South Seas or Pacific Oceans*. He and his wife Sarah were popular with the Lambs, being fanatical whist players. They had a son, 'begotten' according to Lamb 'upon a mermaid'. Robert Southey, soon to be the poet laureate, described Martin as 'the queerest fish out of water'. Martin was disfigured; some sort of childhood paralysis had caused one side of his face to grow larger than the other. He was hot-tempered and argumentative and was once spotted, on a street corner, tempestuously debating the relative merits of Hogarth and Raphael. Charles put him on the 'top scale' of his 'friendship ladder'. Another frequent guest was the newspaper editor, Leigh Hunt. Described by one gushing female as 'fascinating, animated, full of cordial amenity and winning to a degree of which I have never seen the parallel', he was very fond of Mary, once addressing her in one of his articles with the words: 'why have I not the art, like the old writers of dedications, of at once loading thee with panegyric and saving the shoulders of thy modesty.'

Other guests included John Rickman who was Secretary to the Speaker in the House of Commons and his clerk and successor, Edward Phillips, who was permanently in debt. Basil Montagu, the illegitimate son of the fourth Earl of Sandwich, also came. He was a barrister whose incautious comments led to a bitter quarrel between Coleridge and Wordsworth. It took all Crabb Robinson's diplomacy to bring about a reconciliation, although the poets never became really close again. The law was also represented by another regular, Barron Field, who lived nearby in the Temple and claimed to be a descendant of Oliver Cromwell. From the world of music came *The Times*'s music reporter, Thomas Alsager, and William Ayrton, the musical director of the King's Theatre. Late in the evening, when the theatres closed, came the playwright James Kenney, the Shakespearean actor Charles Kemble, brother of Mrs Siddons, the comedian John Liston and the actress Fanny Kelly.

According to Talfourd, the 'sedater part of the company' came early, then, at around ten o'clock, the 'happier stragglers' dropped in from the play to be greeted by Mary and Charles. They were good hosts, making an excellent double act in which Charles talked – Hazlitt said Lamb 'always made the best pun and the best remark in the course of the evening ... No one ever stammered out such fine, piquant, deep, eloquent things in half a dozen half-sentences as he does' – and Mary listened. 'She was oftener a listener than a speaker' according to Charles Cowden Clarke, a young friend and admirer of the Lambs. Mary, he said, was 'ever a chosen source of confidence among her friends, who turned to her for consolation, confirmation, and advice, in matters of nicest moment, always secure of deriving from her both aid and solace'. Crabb

Robinson said, 'With her I can unbosom myself cordially.' He enjoyed their 'confidential gossiping'. Mary never fell out with anyone herself and she was skilled at smoothing over difficulties and making people feel comfortable. Thomas de Quincey describes her as being 'pointedly kind and conciliatory in her manner' to him. She had a knack, she herself said, 'of looking into people's real characters and never expecting them to act out of it – never expecting another to do as I would in the same case'. Perhaps she always remembered that she had once been deserving of the harshest judgement and been treated with love instead. But her uncritical affection, always giving people the benefit of the doubt, was an endearing quality and it won and kept her many friends. When Crabb Robinson decided he had had enough of Hazlitt's rudeness and was going to cut Hazlitt, Mary told him calmly, 'you are rich in friends. We cannot afford to cast off ours because they are not all we wish.' She was no fair-weather friend either. When Leigh Hunt was sentenced to two years' imprisonment in 1813 for libelling the Prince Regent, she and Charles were among his most constant visitors. Hunt recalled that the brother and sister 'came to comfort me in all weathers, hail or sunshine, in day-light or in darkness, even in the dreadful frost and snow at the beginning of 1814. I am always afraid of talking about them, lest my tropical temperament should seem to render me too florid.' And when Martin Burney scandalised his family by revealing that he'd been secretly married to a servant girl for five years, Mary was his most loyal champion. Crabb Robinson, like most of Burney's friends, thought the wife was 'a low person' and he admired Mary's kindness in taking her under her protection.

Hospitality at the Lambs' parties was simple, unpretentious and generous. Mary directed the servant Becky to spread plates of cold roast lamb or boiled beef and roast potatoes out on the side table and then urged their guests to help themselves.

The Lambs' veal pie was immortalised in a pun from Edward Phillips. 'That's game,' he called as Martin Burney muttered a quotation over the last few slices. Drink was porter sent from one of the many nearby Fleet Street taverns. When it ran out, they sent Becky out for some more. She had been with William Hazlitt before she joined the Lambs and was largely responsible for any order that existed in the Lambs' rackety household. She watched the finances carefully, kept them from being imposed upon by tradesmen and bossed them about.

The card table was laid out at the start of the evening. Both Mary and Charles had a passion for cards, a pastime that was typical of the age they lived in. The Regency period was notorious for gambling; in social circles considerably higher than the Lambs, men and women lost thousands of pounds at all-night card games. Mary once anticipated a happy week's holiday with the words, 'I intend to read Novels and play at piquet all day long.' As well as piquet, the Lambs liked whist and Mary was intensely fond of cribbage. 'It was not "silent whist",' said Proctor. 'The game was enlivened by sundry brief ejaculations and pungent questions, which kept alive the wits of the party present.' You could play or not as it suited you. Leigh Hunt called Charles's evenings 'humanity's triumph; for whist players and no whist-players there for the first time met together. Talk not to me of great houses in which such things occur; for there the whist-players are gamblers, and the no whist-players are nobody at all. Here, the whist was for its own sake, and yet the non-players were tolerated.'

Once the game was over, punch – made by Mary – and brandy and water were produced and, with the hard drinking came heavy smoking and intense conversations. Proctor claimed that he never heard, in all his life, 'so much unpretending good sense, as at Charles Lamb's social parties. Often, a piece of sparkling humour was shot out that illuminated the whole evening. Sometimes there was a flight of high and earnest talk, that took one half way towards the stars.' Talfourd said that the topics were 'chiefly sought among the obscure and remote; the odd, the quaint, the fantastic were drawn out from their dusty recesses. Whatever the subject, 'it was always discussed by those best entitled to talk on it; no others had a chance of being heard. This remarkable freedom from bores was produced in Lamb's circle by the authoritative texture of its commanding minds.' Hazlitt, in his essay, 'On the Conversation of Authors', based on memories of the Lambs' evenings, waxed ecstatic: 'How often did we cut into the haunch of letters, while we discussed the haunch of mutton on the table! How we skimmed the cream of criticism! How we got into the heart of controversy! How we picked out the marrow of authors! And, in our flowing cups, many a good name and true was freshly remembered.'

Guests came, not just for the card games and the good talk but also because the Lambs' informal salon was one of the places where the literary lions assembled. Wordsworth came and held court, talking of poetry and allowing himself to be persuaded to read his own poetry aloud. Coleridge could always be counted on to make an impression, delivering monologues that alternately puzzled and delighted his listeners. Talfourd said that when 'Coleridge came, argument, wit, humour, criticism were hushed, the pertest, smartest, and the cleverest felt that all were assembled to listen: and if a card-table had been filled, or a dispute begun before he was excited to continuous speech, his gentle voice, undulating in music, soon "suspended whist and took with ravishment / The thronging audience".' Henry Crabb Robinson, on the other hand, frequently described the poet as 'uninteresting'. And Hazlitt was even more dismissive. Coleridge, he wrote, was 'the only person who can talk to all sorts of people, on all sorts of subjects, without caring a farthing for their understanding one word he says – and he talks only for admiration and to be listened to, and accordingly the least interruption puts him out ... I firmly believe he would make just the same impression on half his audiences, if he purposely repeated absolute nonsense with the same voice and manner and inexhaustible flow of undulating speech!'

The two poets were the star attractions and neither was too grand to refuse to perform for their audience. They even indulged in a little competitiveness. Henry Crabb Robinson wrote of arriving at the Lambs' to find 'a large party collected round the two poets, but Coleridge had the larger body. Talfourd only had fixed himself by Wordsworth and remained by his side all the evening. There was however, scarcely any conversation beyond a whisper. Coleridge was philosophising in his rambling way to Monkhouse, who listened attentively; to Manning who sometimes smiled as if he thought Coleridge had no right to metaphysicise on chemistry without any knowledge on the subject; to Martin Burney who was eager to interpose, and Alsager, who was content to be a listener; while Wordsworth was for a great part of the time engaged tête-à-tête with Talfourd, I could catch scarcely anything of the conversation; but I heard at one time Coleridge quoting Wordworth's verses, and Wordsworth quoting – not Coleridge's but his own ...'

On other nights, the talk was more general. There were fond reminiscences. 'We had a good cheerful meeting on Wednesday,' Mary once wrote. 'Much talk of Winterslow, its woods and its sunflowers.' They caught up with each other's news. 'Rickman has got a better place ... and Phillips the card player has succeeded him ... There has arisen a feud between Hazlitt and Captain Burney ... Kenny has one more child and a successful farce. Martin Burney is going to write a successful tragedy. Godwin has just published a new book, I wish it may be successful but I am sure it is very dull,' noted Mary after one Thursday night. There was gossip or, as Proctor put it, 'anecdotes, characteristic, showing the strong and weak points of human nature'. There was plenty of malice and disparagement of others. Talfourd spoke of 'the tendency, often more idle than malicious, to soften down the intellectual claims of the absent, which so insidiously besets literary conversation, and teaches a superficial insincerity, even to substantial esteem and regard, and which was sometimes insinuated into the conversation of Lamb's friends.'

The group teased each other and fell out with each other and then usually made it up and, even if they didn't, their annoyance never stopped them from coming to the Lambs'. Quarrels, many no doubt fuelled by brandy, were plentiful. Crabb Robinson disliked Leigh Hunt and his wife and disapproved of Martin Burney's irregular lifestyle – 'he wants manners to make him agreeable, and morals to make him respectable'. Southey grumbled that Wordsworth thought too highly of his own poetry; Hunt did a good, mocking imitation of Hazlitt; Hazlitt once quarrelled so badly with John Lamb over the use of colours in Holbein and Vandyke that John Lamb knocked Hazlitt to the floor. Hazlitt then got up and said he would forgive him and added, 'I am a metaphysician and do not mind a blow; nothing but an *idea* hurts me.'

For Mary and Charles, this group of acrimonious, loving, clever people, with their fierce loyalties and frequent sulks and squabbles, functioned like an extended, alternative family. They had no children and their brother John, although he married and his wife had children from her previous marriage, seemed in his solipsism and self-containment to be the eternal bachelor. This network of friends was of vital importance; without outside influences, Mary and Charles found their relationship too intense and suffocating. Even in company, they were tense and alert to each other. According to Cowden Clarke, 'She had a way of repeating her brother's words assentingly when he spoke to her.' Their antennae were tuned to pick up each other's weaknesses. Cowden Clarke often noticed on Mary's face 'an upward look of peculiar meaning, when directed towards him, as though to give him assurance that all was then well with her'. Talfourd recalled that, 'If, in company, he perceived she looked languid, he would repeatedly ask her, "Mary, does your head ache?" "Don't you feel unwell?" and would be satisfied by none of her gentle assurances, that his fears were groundless.' He also noticed how Mary, in between her hostess duties, watched her brother, 'turning, now and then, an anxious loving eye on Charles, which is softened into a half-humorous expression of resignation to inevitable fate, as he mixes his second tumbler!'

The painter Matilda Betham recalled how they worked together: 'When I knew him first, I happened to sit next him at dinner, and he was running on about some lady who had died of love for him, saying, "he was very sorry," but we could not command such inclinations, making all the common-place stuff said on such occasions appear very ridiculous; his sister laughingly interrupting him now and then, by saying "why she's alive now!" "why she's married, and has a large family etc". He would not, however allow it, and went on.' He was the wit, she was the straight man, feeding him his lines.

Although they both loved and needed these evenings, they worried about the effect they had on their lives and work. Charles, in particular, fretted that the number of interruptions meant that he couldn't work, which made the surprise discovery of some extra rooms in their apartment all the more welcome. Mary told Matilda's younger sister Barbara Betham how the cries of a cat led them to force the lock on a little room at the top of the kitchen stairs. Behind it were 'four untenanted, unowned rooms'. They moved into them gradually, 'first putting up lines to dry our clothes, then moving my brother's bed into one of these more commodious than his own room'. Charles intended to use one of them as his study, a bit of privacy away from the frequent 'kind interruptions of friends'. A few hours in there and Charles was back downstairs complaining that he 'could do nothing . . . with those bare whitewashed walls before his eyes. He could not write in that dull unfurnished prison.'

When Charles was away at the office the following day, Mary set to work to make the room more comfortable. 'I gathered up various bits of old carpeting to cover the floor; and to a little break the blank look of the bare walls, I hung up a few old prints that used to ornament the kitchen.' On Charles's return, he caught her excitement and the two of them cut prints out of books and used them to cover the walls. 'He cut out every print from every book in his old library, coming every now and then to ask my leave to strip a fresh poor author – which he might not do, you know, without my permission, as I am elder sister. There was such pasting, such consultation where portraits, and where the series of pictures of Ovid, Milton, and Shakespeare would show to most advantage, and in what obscure corner authors of humbler note might be allowed to tell their stories.' The result was that the 'poor despised garret' became 'the print room' and their 'favourite sitting room'.

Still the people kept coming and, in truth, neither Mary nor Charles really wanted any change; they would not have known what to do with solitude. But the parties wore Mary out and, she believed, increased the chances of her madness returning. In 1814, they cut the parties down to once a month, believing it would be better for her health, but they could not give them up entirely. When, years later, William Hazlitt published his essay 'On the Conversation of Authors', an account of the Thursday nights at the Lambs, it gave her 'unmixed delight'. Not only did she enjoy the parties, each one was a joyous mark of how far she had travelled since the days when she'd been a seamstress with nothing to look forward to but hard work and ill health. She recalled those days in an essay entitled 'On Needlework', written in December 1814 for the *British Lady's Magazine* and it afforded her a unique opportunity to reflect on her own experiences and to take stock of the way her life had changed.

She could have delivered a diatribe against the appalling conditions of sewing work, painting a harrowing portrait of young girls ruining their health in a futile attempt to support themselves and then winding up with a heartfelt appeal for charity on their behalf. But Mary had learned her trade well while writing for Godwin's Juvenile Library. She knew how to write for her market and, appreciating the magazine's middle-class readership, she made instead a cogent benefits-for-all argument that flattered her readers' intelligence and appealed to their common sense and intellectual vanity. While women who didn't need to sewed, then women who *did* need to suffered.

'To lighten the heavy burden which many ladies impose upon themselves is one object which I have in view; but, I confess, my strongest motive is to excite attention towards the industrious sisterhood to which I once belonged,' is how she began. She went on to argue that, by making a hobby of a business, the woman of means tied herself up in wearying labour and simultaneously drove down the prices that a seamstress could charge. 'I affirm that I know not a single family where there is not some essential drawback to its comfort which may be traced to needlework done at home, as the phrase is for all needlework performed in a family by some of its own members, and for which no remuneration in money is received or expected.'

She was, she wrote, convinced that it would be better for everyone if needlework was only ever practised for money. And such an arrangement, she argued boldly, would help place women 'upon an equality with men, as far as respects the mere enjoyment of life'.

'They can do what they like,' we say. Do not these words generally mean, they have time to seek out whatever amusements suit their tastes? We dare not tell them we have no time to do this; for, if they should ask in what manner we dispose of our time, we should blush to enter upon a detail of the minutiae which compose the sum of a woman's daily employment. Nay, many a lady who allows not herself one quarter of an hour's positive leisure during her waking hours, considers her own husband as the most industrious of men, if he steadily pursue his occupation till the hour of dinner, and will be perpetually lamenting her own idleness.

Real business and real leisure make up the portions of men's time – two sources of happiness which we certainly partake of in a very inferior degree.

The essay, a deft mixture of the conservative and the radical, took the argument right into the heart of the relationship between men and women. 'The highest praise we can aim at is to be accounted the helpmates of man,' she wrote. Mary Lamb was no feminist but she was angered by the suffering of sewing women and enraged by the sight of women wasting time and energy on work that someone else could do better and to their profit. It was preferable, she stated firmly, to abandon sewing entirely and thereby add to 'the slender gains of the corset-maker, the milliner, the dress-maker, the plain-worker, the embroidress, and all the numerous classifications of females supporting themselves by needle-work, that great staple commodity which is alone appropriated to the self-supporting part of our sex'.

She accepted that many parents assumed their daughters would marry and so decided not to educate them properly but what about the girls who remained single, she wanted to know. Why can't they have some of the jobs currently done by men? 'If at the birth of girls it were possible to foresee in what cases it would be their fortune to pass a single life, we should soon find trades wrested from their present occupiers and trans-ferred to the exclusive possession of our sex,' she wrote. 'The whole mechanical business of copying writings in the law department, for instance, might very soon be transferred with advantage to the poorer sort of women, who with very little teaching would soon beat their rivals of the other sex in facility and neatness. The parents of female children, who were known to be destined from their birth to maintain themselves through the whole course of their lives with like certainty as their sons are, would feel it a duty incumbent on themselves to strengthen the minds, and even the bodily constitutions of their girls, so circumstanced, by an education which, without affronting the preconceived habits of society, might enable them to follow some occupation now considered above the capacity or too robust for the constitution of our sex.'

Briefly, she let herself dwell on the possibility of choice and opportunity. 'Plenty of resources would then lie open for single women to obtain an independent livelihood.' After this, Mary's statement that learning a trade might cause a girl to lose her expectation of aspiring to the 'condition of a happy English wife', looks more than a little disingenuous.

She attacked the Protestant notion of thrift:

'A penny saved is a penny earned,' is a maxim not true, unless the penny be saved in the same time in which it might have been earned. I who have known what it is to work for money earned, have since had much experience in working for money saved; and I consider from the closest calculation I can make that a penny saved in that way bears about a true proportion to a farthing earned.

. . . It would be an excellent plan, attended with very little trouble, to calculate every evening how much money has been saved by needlework done in the family, and compare the result with the daily portion of the yearly income. Nor would it be amiss to make a memorandum of the time passed in this way, adding also a guess as to what share it has taken up in the thoughts and conversation. This would be an easy mode of forming a true notion, and getting at the exact worth of this species of home industry, and perhaps might place it in a different light from that in which it has hitherto been the fashion to consider it.

She was speaking out, boldly, telling the truth about female labour, both paid and unpaid. 'Needlework, taken up as an amusement, may not be altogether unamusing,' she wrote, sweetly damning the pastime with faint praise but, 'let us not confuse the motives of economy with those of simply pastime. If a lady finds needlework so enjoyable, let her do the old fashioned work – knitting, knotting, carpet working, and the like ingenious pursuits – those so-often praised but tedious works.' But when it comes to sewing clothes, let her follow her conscience and 'give the money so saved to poor needlewomen belonging to those branches of employment from which she has borrowed these shares of pleasurable labour'.

More than two decades and a whole world of experience

lay between the writer Mary Lamb who wrote this essay and the Mary who slaved away as a seamstress, but she had not forgotten her earlier self. She claimed that writing the article caused her 'great fatigue' – perhaps she was wearied by the painful memories it raised – but, when she wrote it, she had the confidence of three books behind her and had spent countless evenings listening to the arguments of the radicals gathered about her own fireside. Although she had herself been liberated from the necessity of earning a living by sewing, she still knew women who hadn't. She had at least one 'young friend' who worked as a mantua maker and she solicited business on her behalf. She brought to the essay personal experience of the misery involved in sewing for a living, a tough, self-educated mind and an awareness of radical ideas concerning the relationship between the sexes. It was the work of a woman in the prime of her life and the full exercise of her intellectual talents. In it she reclaimed her past, made political sense of it, practical use of it and then sent it off to where it might do some good.

Shortly after the essay's publication, the personal politics at her own Thursday night parties reached boiling point. On 22 June 1815, the news came that the Battle of Waterloo had put paid to all Napoleon's ambitions and the whole of England rejoiced – but many of the friends who gathered in Mary's home were distraught. Godwin had wanted a French victory and Henry Crabb Robinson, normally the most suave of men, quarrelled bitterly with him. Hazlitt, the husband of Mary's old friend, Sarah, was driven almost mad by the defeat of Napoleon. He wandered the streets, drunk, unwashed and unshaven, and quarrelled with almost everyone. He enraged Crabb Robinson who called him 'overbearing and rude . . . He mixes passion and ill-humour and personal feelings in his judgements on public events and characters more than any man I know, and this infinitely detracts from the value of his opinions, which, possessing as he does rare talents, would be otherwise very valuable.' Hazlitt's support for Napoleon, he dismissed, erroneously, as bloody-mindedness. 'He always vindicates Buonaparte, not because he is insensible to his enormous crimes, but out of spite to the Tories of this country.'

Amidst this turmoil, there was not much chance of the 'absolute quiet' her brother told Dorothy Wordsworth that she needed. Dorothy Wordsworth wrote that Charles was constantly anxious about Mary's health: 'everything out of the common course of her own daily life caused excitement and agitation equally injurious to her,' she said. 'Charles speaks of the necessity of absolute quiet and at the same time of being obliged sometimes to have company that they would be better without.' Absolute quiet may have been a necessity but so too was going out. Mary was a natural born gadabout. These evenings were just part of her social life. She went to other people's houses frequently, attended the theatre regularly, played cards for long hours late into the night. Henry Crabb Robinson's diary shows how busy was her social life. A typical series of entries in early 1815 shows how little she heeded any requirements for rest. On the 19th, Crabb Robinson met Mary, newly recovered and out of the asylum, 'pale and thin, but in no respect alarmingly'. A week later he met her again at a dinner party where Charles got very drunk. Two days after that, he ran into her again at the Godwins'. Four days later, she went to the theatre with him. Meanwhile, Charles wrote plaintively about the need for solitude. 'She is . . . too much harassed by Company, who cannot or will not see how late hours and society teaze her.' But the parties, the hectic socialising were all part of Mary's brave bid for a normal life; a desire to cram the time between her illness with as much life and activity and enjoyment as possible. She knew her period of liberty would inevitably end and that she would be banished again so, while she could, she seized the day and, even more so, the nights.

The regular holidays were part of the same drive, the desire to accumulate experience and pleasures while she could. She was enthusiastic about Cambridge when she and Charles visited in August that year. 'In my life I never spent so many pleasant hours together as I did at Cambridge.' She thrilled to the Cathedral service at King's College Chapel and decided she liked the 'little gloomy colleges' best; 'I felt as if I could live and die in them and never wish to speak again.' They looked at the colleges where her favourites, Coleridge and Manning, had studied. In May 1815, she took a jaunt to Mackery End,

The house at Mackery End.

in Hertfordshire, back into her past with her brother and his friend Barron Field. Here she'd spent her summers as a child; here she'd revisited in memory when she wrote, 'The Farmhouse' in *Mrs Leicester's School*. Now she revisited it in real life, spending the Whitsun break walking in the old well-loved neighbourhood. Charles, she wrote to a friend, that onetime 'urchin of three or four years' had become her 'lord and master' who hung back and 'refused leave to enter' the house until she 'overcame his scruples'. Then 'three or four dogs barking at me enough to frighten me from any other farmhouse in England did not deter me from going in by myself,' she went on. 'I found no soul of a large family I had left there, a granddaughter of my aunt's not then born received me in a most friendly manner, sent her husband to fetch in Charles and Field and immediately began to call us Charles and Mary with most cousin-like familiarity. Not only all the inhabitants I knew were gone, some to their graves and some to their husbands, but the old house was rebuilt. Yet the orchard the farm yard and the garden remained.' So the places she had cared most about were still there and these relatives were connected to her through the mother she had killed and yet she could still visit them and be welcomed by them. The effect on her was profound; she wrote: 'Charles says he never saw me look so happy in his life, and he was not much less so for in the evening he said it was the pleasantest day he ever had in his life.'

She was ill in the autumn, worryingly soon after her last bout of madness. That and the happiness they'd felt while rusticating gave them more reason to entertain in earnest the Londoner's perennial fantasy about escaping into a rural idyll. In the summer of 1816, they took lodgings in the village of Dalston. For ten weeks, Mary said, they 'obtained a very clear idea of the great benefit of quiet – of early hours and time entirely at one's own disposal'. It all made sense but what London had to offer was better than sense. 'The return to old friends – the sight of old familiar faces round me has almost reconciled me to occasional headaches and fits of peevish weariness,' she continued. She thought they 'could live in the country entirely' were it not for the fact that she wished to 'live and die in the Temple' where she was born.

Their move when it came was not to the country. Instead, in October of the following year, they left their beloved Temple – the 'rooms were dirty and out of repair and the inconveniences of living in chambers became every year more irksome' – explained Mary, and moved to Covent Garden, the heart of the theatre district and one of the busiest parts of London. The quiet life could wait a little longer. Their old home had 'sheltered' them but their new one was like stepping into another, rawer world. Covent Garden acted on Mary's sensitive nerves like a drink of champagne. She wrote to Dorothy Wordsworth a letter that bubbled with enthusiasm. Covent Garden was 'a place all alive with noise and bustle, Drury Lane Theatre in sight from our front and Covent Garden from our back windows. The hubbub of the carriages returning from the play does not annoy me in the least – strange that it does not, for it is quite tremendous. I quite enjoy looking out of the window and listening to the calling up of the carriages and the squabbles of the coachmen and linkboys.' The visitors continued to come to Covent Garden and, although Mary believed that she was forced to pay a high price for her lively social life in the form of mental breakdown, she clearly thought it a price worth paying.

Chapter 11

Fanny

A female poet, or female author of any kind, ranks
below an actress, I think.
Charles Lamb, 1826

AMONG THE LAMBS' REGULAR visitors was the actress
Fanny Kelly. Both Mary and Charles liked her and she
was popular with all their friends. Henry Crabb Robinson
described her as 'neither young nor handsome, but very agreeable, her voice and manner those of a person who knows her
own worth, but is, at the same time, not desirous to assume
upon it. She talks like a sensible woman.' He thought her an
'unaffected, sensible, clear-headed, warm-hearted woman; she
has none of the vanities or arrogance of the actress'. Like Mary,
Fanny was intelligent but she had only been partially educated.
Mary gave her lessons in Latin and admired her tremendously;
she thought she was an 'excellent actress' and once pointed
her out to a young friend with the words, 'Look at her well
. . . for she is a woman to remember having seen.' When Mary
read a less than glowing review of the young actress's performance while on tour in Scotland, she wrote to her consolingly
and sympathetically. 'If those cold northern people do not
appear quite to estimate your powers of giving pleasure, you

Fanny Kelly by Thomas Uwins.

are soon coming home, where one or two at least know how to value them.' Mary was one and Charles was two but, in fact, he did more than just admire Fanny Kelly.

In 1818, he published his *Works*, a collection of poems (some – 'Dialogue between a Mother and Child', 'Salome' and the Da Vinci poems – by Mary), essays and the plays *Rosamund Gray*, *John Woodvil* and *Mr H*. It also included the following sonnet.

> You are not, Kelly, of the common strain,
> That stoop their pride and female honour down
> To please that many-headed beast the town,
> And vend their lavish smiles and tricks for gain;
> By fortune thrown amid the actor's train,
> You keep your native dignity of thought;
> The plaudits that attend you come unsought,
> As tributes due unto your natural vein.
> Your tears have passion in them, and a grace
> Of genuine freshness, which our hearts avow;
> Your smiles are winds whose ways we cannot trace,
> That vanish and return we know not how –
> And please the better from a pensive face,
> A thoughtful eye and a reflecting brow.

He was keen to draw Fanny's attention to the poem; when the collection came out in August, he sent her a copy with a note: 'Mr Lamb having taken the liberty of addressing a slight compliment to Miss Kelly in his first volume, respectfully requests her acceptance of the collection.'

Frances Maria Kelly was one of fourteen children; their father, Thomas Kelly had worked as a wine merchant in Dublin during the day, and at night transformed himself into a Master of the Mask and Revels. Their Uncle Michael was a composer and singer. All the children were musical, some acted as well. Fanny's sister Lydia was an actress too and her sister Nancy married a famous comedian.

Fanny made her first stage appearance at the age of seven, and when she turned sixteen began her theatrical apprenticeship on that gruelling and testing round of performances known as repertory theatre, touring England, performing in venues that included theatre halls, barns and fairgrounds. In 1799, she became a member of the Drury Lane Company, still the Lambs' favourite theatre despite the fact that *Mr H* had flopped so resoundingly there. When she joined, the actresses Dora Jordan (mistress of the Duke of Clarence, later William IV) and Sarah Siddons (who Mary's mother had supposedly looked like) held sway there. Although she was never in their league, she was none the less attractive, vibrant and popular with colleagues and audiences alike. The comedian Oxberry, who published his *Dramatic Biography and Histrionic Anecdotes* in 1825, had this to say about her: 'Miss Kelly is in person about the common size; her figure is symmetrically beautiful, her face is round and pleasing, though not handsome; her eyes are light blue; her forehead is peculiarly low, and this circumstance materially mars the effect of her countenance; her smile is exceedingly beautiful, and may be said to completely sun her countenance.' In a footnote, he added rather censoriously, 'By the bye, this lady is by far too fond of sporting her shape in male attire; but we are tired with quarrelling with actresses on this account.'

Perhaps Fanny knew that her 'symmetrically beautiful' figure was best displayed in men's clothes and so made a speciality of taking on boys' parts; she had been the Duke of York in *Richard III*. But she was also Lucy in Gay's *The Beggar's Opera* and the young servant girl, Annette, unjustly accused of stealing jewellery in *The Maid and the Magpie*. She frequently played Ophelia to the impassioned Edmund Kean's Hamlet. Byron was a fan of her acting, the Duke of Devonshire admired her and she'd sent the Earl of Essex off with a flea in his ear when he offered to make her his mistress. Her stinging letter of rebuke – 'nothing shall prevail upon me again to expose myself to what every well regulated mind must consider in the light of an insult' – was a masterpiece of outraged dignity and disgust.

She was as brave as she was talented. In 1816, a lunatic called George Barnett who was obsessed with actresses who played men's roles stalked her. In February 1816, he sent her a deranged letter, demanding that she marry him:

> ... I think my good intentions towards you have been more trifled with than any of my contemporaries. My claim to your person is therefore greater, which determines me to demand your hand, or in other words, to make you my wife.
>
> You will either consent to this or accept my challenge. I will attend you any hour you please on Wednesday or before.
>
> I have witnessed your dexterity in firing a Gun, but suppose a Pistol will better suit you as being much lighter.
>
> Had you not infringed the rights of your sex, I should not have thus address'd you; but as it is, no other Person can better this letter than yourself. I shall not brook contempt or trifling excuses.

Fanny ignored this letter and the other one – wilder still – that he sent four days later. This time, the tone was even more threatening as he ended: 'I love the sex, and once esteemed you as an ornament to it, till you raised my indignation by your impertinence and scandalous abuses. You are very partial to a disguised Male Dress, but let me not experience any more of your folly, for if I do, I will secure you as an Imposter and punish you for your temerity.'

Throughout this week, Fanny Kelly carried on working. She was Annette in *The Maid and the Magpie* on Wednesday, put on boys' clothes to play William in *Rosina* on Friday, and on Saturday she made her appearance as Nan in *Modern Antiques*. Mary and Charles were in the audience. Halfway through the first act of *Modern Antiques*, Fanny's mad admirer jumped to his feet, waved a duelling pistol in the air and then fired. Fanny collapsed, her co-star caught her and the bullet ricocheted back into the auditorium. Until Fanny reappeared on stage to show her audience that she was unharmed, neither Mary nor her brother knew what had happened to their friend. It was a frightening incident and Fanny's response was impressive.

Charles was more than impressed. He talked of Fanny Kelly's 'divine plain face'. She affected him powerfully, though for some time he spoke as if it was merely her acting that fascinated him. He used his role as theatre critic to draw attention to her performances. He railed in print against the theatre managers who didn't give her a part in a new play, *A Word for the Ladies*, writing in the *Examiner*: 'It was not without a feeling of pain, that we observed Miss Kelly among the spectators on the first night of the new comedy. What does she do before the curtain? She should have been on the stage. With such youth, such talents, – Those powers of pleasing, with that will to please, it is too much that she should be forgotten, discarded, laid aside like an old fashion. It really is not yet the season for her "among the wastes of time to go". Is it Mr Stephen Kemble, or the Sub-Committee; or what heavy body is it, which interposes itself between us and this light of the stage.'

He couldn't leave the subject of Fanny Kelly alone. In January

1819, he wrote to his friend Matthew Gutch in Bristol, urging him to make a point of seeing her act when she appeared there. His entire letter was taken up with her. Her method of acting was 'the joy of a freed spirit, escaping from care', her smiles 'seemed saved out of the fire, relics which a good and innocent heart had snatched up as most portable'. She was 'no ordinary tragedian' and in comedy, too, she was delightful. Even when her performances fell short, this was due, in Charles's opinion, to her deeper merit. 'She does not succeed in what are called fine lady parts. Our friend C. once observed, that no man of genius ever figured as a gentleman. Neither did any woman, gifted with Mrs Jordan's or Miss Kelly's sensibilities, ever taken upon herself to shine as a fine lady, the very essence of this character consisting in the entire repression of all genius and all feeling.' He realised, belatedly, how much he was giving away about his feelings. 'I should apologise for the length of this letter, if I did not remember the lively interest you used to take in theatrical performances,' he concluded his letter in a sentence that could have fooled nobody.

To Fanny Kelly herself, he wrote, as well as sonnets, teasing letters about theatre tickets, making a pun on the words 'bones' i.e. free passes to the theatre. 'If your Bones are not engaged on Monday night, will you favour us with the use of them? I know, if you can oblige us, you will make no bones of it; if you cannot, it shall break none betwixt us. We might ask somebody else, but we do not like the bones of any strange animals.'

In July 1819, he wrote a review of *The Jovial Crew* in which Fanny was appearing, a review which, quite unashamedly, mixed the personal with the critical. In fact, he raved about her: 'Her tones, such as we have heard by the side of old woods, when an irresistible face has come peeping on one on a sudden; with her full black locks, and a voice – how shall we describe it? – a voice that was by nature meant to convey nothing but truth and goodness ...' On and on he enthuses: 'Those ballad-singer's notes', 'her face, with a wild out-of-doors grace upon it'. He finishes: '"What a lass that were," said a stranger who sate beside us, speaking of Miss Kelly in Rachel, "to go a gypsying through the world with ..."'

Just over a fortnight later, he sat down and spelled out his wishes clearly; he made the actress a formal offer of marriage. He began by expressing his pleasure at a recent performance of hers, a pleasure that was mixed with pain. 'What a task for you to undergo! At a time when your heart is sore from real sorrow! It has given rise to a train of thinking, which I cannot suppress.'

In the second paragraph, he made his offer: 'Would to God you were released from this way of life; that you could bring your mind to consent to take your lot with us, and throw off for ever the whole burden of your Profession.' He wanted her to take her time in thinking his offer over and then he made it clear that he had considered the practicalities. 'I have quite income enough, if that were all, to justify for me making such a proposal, with what I may call even a handsome provision for my survivor. What you possess of your own would naturally be appropriated to those, for whose sakes chiefly you have made so many hard sacrifices.'

The business matters dealt with, he continued: 'I am not so foolish as not to know that I am a most unworthy match for such a one as you, but you have for years been a principal object in my mind. In many a sweet assumed character I have learned to love you, but simply as F.M. Kelly I love you better than them all.' The artist in him responded to her acting.

'Can you quit these shadows of existence, and come and be a reality to us? Can you leave off harassing yourself to please a thankless multitude, who know nothing of you, and begin at last to live to yourself & your friends?'

He was caught up with her performances, imagining her accepting or rejecting a suitor in a play. 'As plainly and frankly as I have seen you give or refuse sent in some feigned scene, so frankly do me the justice to answer me.' He was far from anticipating consent. 'It is impossible I should feel injured or aggrieved by your telling me at once, that the proposal does not suit you.'

Even in this love letter, Mary was not far from his thoughts. There would be no separation on his part from his sister; at times he seemed to be proposing on Mary's behalf as well as his own. Fanny was being invited to join the two of them: 'Happier, far happier, could I have leave to hope a time might come, when our friends might be your friends; our interest yours.'

He was offering her not just love but also 'book-knowledge' – his and Mary's book knowledge, writing: 'If in that inconsiderable particular we have any little advantage, might impart something to you, which you would every day have it in your power ten thousand fold to repay by the added cheerfulness and joy which you could not fail to bring as a dowry into whatever family should have the honour and happiness of receiving you.' He signed the letter (disingenuously) 'in haste' and (sincerely) 'with entire respect and deepest affection'.

Did Mary know that he was making the proposal? Although he wrote 'we' and 'our' he might have been assuming that his sister would agree with him, that whatever he wanted, she would go along with. Perhaps he thought he'd get his acceptance and then face whatever music there was at home afterwards. He may have expected a refusal. If he did tell Mary, she must have waited for Fanny's answer with as much nervousness as he did. If Fanny said yes, their – her – way of life would change for ever. There would be another person whose needs, feelings and wishes would have to be accommodated in the tight relationship she and Charles had formed. She would have to share her brother, his home, his income, his care. For, as Charles's love letter showed, there was a strong streak of protectiveness in his attitude to Fanny. He saw himself as her rescuer; in the past such feelings had always been exclusively for Mary. She had grown up in a household where wife and sister-in-law fought. More than ten years earlier, she had written wise words to Sarah Stoddart on the very subject, a letter in which she boasted of her own ability to cope with such a situation. 'I think myself the only woman in the world, who could live with a brother's wife, and make a real friend of her.' Now she might get the chance to follow her own advice. 'Tell her every thing that passes,' she had told Sarah. 'Show her all your letters.' In Mary's case, that would have meant Fanny knowing everything about her, becoming a witness to her bouts of mania, seeing her when she was in the depths of depression.

Fanny Kelly did not keep them waiting for long. Her letter was dated a day after his. It was kindly written but it was, unmistakably, a refusal.

An early and deeply rooted attachment has fixed my heart on one from whom no worldly prospect can well induce me to withdraw it, but while I thus frankly and decidedly decline your proposal, believe me, I am not insensible to the high honour which the preference of such a mind as yours confers upon me – let me, however, hope that all thought upon this subject will end with this letter, and that you will henceforth encourage no other sentiment towards me than esteem in my private character and a continuance of that approbation of my humble talents which you have already expressed so much and so often to my advantage and gratification.

Twenty-four hours of suspense for Mary and Charles were over. There was to be no gypsying through the world with a new companion for Charles Lamb. He would have to stay put with his old lass at home. He took his rejection calmly, covering up his deeper feelings in his usual way, replying to her letter with good humour and a pun: 'Let what has past "break no bones" between us. You will not refuse us them next time we send for them.'

In August, he reviewed her performance – and, at the same time, his failed suit – when she appeared in *The Hypocrite*. 'She is in truth not framed to tease or torment even in jest, but to utter a heart Yes or No; to yield or refuse assent with a noble sincerity,' he wrote in the *Examiner*. 'We have not the pleasure of being acquainted with her, but we have been told that she carries the same cordial manners into private life.'

Fanny Kelly was a woman of tact; she let him down gently, softening what she really thought. In a letter to her sister Lydia, ten days after refusing Charles, she explained her mind more fully. 'I was indeed sorry to refuse him, for he shows the most tender and loyal affections. But even at the peril of my decision causing him great despondency, which I rather feared, I could have no other course than to say the truth that I could not accept his offer, I could not give my assent to a proposal which would bring me into that atmosphere of sad mental uncertainty which surrounds his domestic life. Marriage might well bring us both added causes for misery and regrets in later years.'

Mary's madness was a problem for Fanny, but even setting that aside, she did not want to marry Charles. She loved the theatre and continued to work as an actress, staying at the Drury Lane Theatre until 1835 when she left to found a drama school, under the patronage of the Duke of Devonshire. There was a mystery about her private life. She either bore or adopted a daughter to whom she left all her property. Charles was deeply attracted to her but he misunderstood her entirely. He had fallen in love with what we today would call a career woman and had failed – gallantly, charmingly but none the less totally – to appreciate what it could mean to an intelligent woman to have work she enjoyed. She loved acting and did it well; he wanted to take her away from it. Fanny Kelly did not want or need to be protected by him.

Despite these undercurrents of emotion, she stayed friendly with Charles and Mary Lamb, remaining one of their most regular visitors. Mary continued to teach her Latin and addressed her as 'my dear friend' in her letters. Charles always carried a torch for her. He wrote her another sonnet when he was inspired by her performance of a blind boy – like her deranged admirer, he was intrigued by her cross-dressing. The sonnet addressed her as a 'celebrated female performer'.

> Rare artist! who with half thy tools or none
> Canst execute with ease thy curious art
> And press thy powerful'st meanings on the heart,
> Unaided by the eye, expression's throne!
> While each blind sense, intelligential grown
> Beyond its sphere, performs the effect of sight:
> Those orbs alone, wanting their proper might,
> All motionless and silent seem to moan
> The unseemly negligence of nature's hand,
> That left them so forlorn. What praise is thine,
> O mistress of the passions; artist fine
> Who dost our souls against our sense command,
> Plucking the horror from a sightless face,
> Lending to blank deformity a grace.

Almost ten years after his proposal, a Mrs Balmanno found herself in the company of Charles and Fanny Kelly and, without knowing their history, picked up on his infatuation. 'Mr Lamb was in high spirits, sauntering about the room, with his hand crossed behind his back, conversing by fits and starts with those most familiarly known to him, but evidently mentally acknowledging Miss Kelly to be the rara avis of his thoughts, by the great attention he paid to every word she uttered.'

When something or someone moved Charles, he wrote about it. He re-created Fanny Kelly's image in his essay 'Barbara S—'. There he wrote of a young actress, scarcely more than a child, working hard, assuming the heavy burden of being the 'sole support' of her family. By mistake, she is paid a whole guinea instead of half a guinea. What will she do? Return it or keep it? 'At that moment a strength not her own, I have heard her say, was revealed to her – a reason above reasoning,' and she hands the overpayment back. 'From that moment a deep peace fell upon her heart, and she knew the quality of honesty . . . I have heard her say that it was a surprise, not much short of mortification to her, to see the coolness with which the old man pocketed the difference, which had caused her such mortal throes.'

It was an appealing story but, even here, Fanny refused Charles. She was a creative artist herself, she shared his understanding of image and the construction of character. In old age, she wrote to her biographer, Charles Kent: 'I perfectly remember relating an incident of my childhood to Charles Lamb and his dear sister, and I have not the least doubt, that the intense interest he seemed to take in the recital, induced him to adopt it as the principal in his beautiful story of "Barbara S—". Much, however, as I venerate the wonderful powers of Charles Lamb as a writer – grateful as I ever must feel to have enjoyed for so many years the friendship of himself and his dear sister, and proudly honoured as I am by the two exquisite sonnets he has given to the world as tributary to my humble talent, I have never been able thoroughly to appreciate the extraordinary skill with which he has, in the construction of his story, desired and contrived so to mystify and characterise the events, as to keep me out of sight, and render it utterly impossible for any one to guess at me as the original heroine.'

She was firm; not denying Charles his right to depict her but taking the opportunity to insist that she should be centre stage. Charles had overwritten her and the artist in her doesn't like it. However much he loved her – and his letter of proposal was very moving – she would have been a bad match for him. He may not have thought so at the time but he was better off with his sister, Mary. She was not to mind being used as raw copy. And besides, there was coming into his life another young girl and one who, unlike the actress, would be willing to brave the 'atmosphere of sad mental uncertainty' and share the Lambs' lives and home.

Chapter 12

Bridget and Emma

His sister, whose literary reputation is associated very closely with her brother's, and who, as the original of 'Bridget Elia,' is a kind of object for literary affection, came in after him.
Nathaniel Parker Willis,
Pencillings By the Way, 1835

THE LAMBS WERE NOW entering a dangerous phase in their lives. Charles was in his mid-forties and Mary was over fifty. He had wanted to get married, which would have meant making the biggest possible change in his life, but it hadn't happened. To wish for change and then have to settle for what you already have can be dismaying and unsettling. He had published *Works*, his choice of title suggesting he saw the two volumes as a summing up of all that he had done and, although much of his work was good, he probably suspected that he was capable of still better. In February 1820, he turned forty-five, often a milestone age. He was restless, fretting about his work at the East India House – 'The Royal Exchange, Gresham's Folly, hath me body and spirit.' Mary too was fretful. They spent the spring of 1820 in the countryside, hoping to find peace of mind, but instead they were bored witless. The garden of their cottage was beautiful, Mary admitted: 'I see every day some new flower peeping out of the ground, and watch its growth; so that I have a sort of an intimate friendship with each. I know the effect of every change of weather upon them – have learned all their names, the duration of their lives, and the whole progress of their domestic economy,' but, and it was an enormous but, 'flowers are flowers still; and I must confess I would rather live in Russell Street all my life, and never set my foot but on the London pavement, than be doomed always to enjoy the silent pleasures I now do. We go to bed at ten o'clock. Late hours are life-shortening things; but I would rather run all risks, and sit every night – at some places I could name – wishing in vain at eleven o'clock for the entrance of the supper tray, than be always up and alive at eight o'clock break-fast, as I am here.'

Charles walked to the office every day and, in his leisure time, burned off his excessive energy with long walks: 'seven-teen miles before dinner,' wrote Mary admiringly. She was fifty-six and finding it hard to keep up with him. A twelve-mile walk – tame by the Lambs' standards – reduced her feet to blisters; 'I by no means perform in this way as well as I used to do,' she admitted.

In July they went to Cambridge where they met up with Crabb Robinson who was on circuit there and went through all their favourite colleges again. And on that visit, they met, for the first time, twelve-year-old Emma Isola. She was a guest at the home of the Lambs' friend, Mrs Paris. Emma was half Italian, the granddaughter of a refugee called Agostino Isola who had taught Wordsworth Italian. Her father, Charles Isola, was a bedell at Cambridge University. She had recently lost her mother and was then living with her aunt, Mrs Humphreys. The Lambs immediately took to her, showing an interest in her welfare that soon outstripped even the great affection they had always shown towards their friends' children.

They invited her to stay with them that Christmas and put a lot of effort into making her welcome and seeing she enjoyed herself. She accompanied them when they went out in the evening; on one occasion, she wrote excitedly to her aunt, they 'did not return till four in the morning'. Charles showed her the lions in the Exeter Exchange and Mary, despite suffering from an attack of rheumatism, treated her to a theatre visit to see *The Antiquary* and a pantomime; both performances 'delighted' the young girl. Her visit was extended past its original deadline; in early January, Charles and Emma wrote a joint letter to her aunt asking for an extension to her holiday. His tone was teasing. 'Emma is a very naughty girl and has broken three cups, one plate and a slop-basin with mere giddiness. She is looking over me, which is impertinent. But if you can spare her longer than her holidays, we shall be happy to keep her, in hopes of her amendment.' He joked that he was teaching her to dance.

Throughout his life, Charles had often added notes to Mary's letters; this was the first time he had done that with anyone else. It was an early but significant indicator of how important Emma was to become to him. Unlike Fanny who had a mind and a career already her own, Emma was more malleable, easier to please, ready to respond to the Lambs' interest in her. She was a delightful new interest in both their lives.

In February 1821, another new person, Bridget Elia, made her first appearance. Bridget Elia was Mary's alter ego, cousin to Elia, under which pseudonym Charles had started writing essays for the *London Magazine*. The Elia essays came about as a result of a perceptive piece of commissioning by the editor John Scott; he saw the real, as yet unexploited talents of Charles and knew how to harness them. The sense of scene that Charles had failed to realise in his plays, the poetic voice that had expressed itself in rather average poems, the humour, the tenderness, were all pressed into play in the Elia essays. They were popular with the *London Magazine*'s readers and Charles was its highest-paid contributor, making Elia professionally as well as creatively the highlight of Charles's life. They are the work on which his posthumous reputation rests. He carried on writing them for the *London Magazine* even after Scott got involved in a stupid quarrel with the editor of another magazine, decided to resolve it by way of a duel and ended up dying of a gunshot wound.

Lamb enjoyed Elia. He played with his identity, finally and joyfully killing him off in a deliciously written piece in which he adopted the guise of 'a friend of the late Elia'. Above all, he *used* him. He liked to tease people with the origin of the Elia name. He claimed to have borrowed it from a deceased colleague of his at South Sea House and insisted that it was pronounced Ellia – with a soft E and a long L. But his friend, the publisher William Hone, said Charles told him it should be pronounced to rhyme with desire, i.e. a liar, and Mary Cowden Clarke recorded that Lamb once told her that 'Elia formed an anagram of "a lie".'

Charles put all his art into the Elia essays and all his heart. He also put himself and his family. In Elia, we find a man whose life story parallels Charles Lamb's. Lamb/Elia attended Christ's Hospital School, worked for the South Sea House, took holidays in Hertfordshire, Margate and Oxford and never married. The two men – the one real, the other fictional – had many attitudes in common: both were whimsical with a fondness for old books and the sweet-toned nostalgia of Elia's was the delicate and haunting echo of what Charles joked was 'a constitutional imbecility' that caused him 'too obstinately to cling to the remembrances of childhood'. Such is the close identification between writer and character that the essays have traditionally been read as pure autobiography, a misreading that both Charles and Elia warned against. Charles described his first Elia essay, 'The South-Sea House', as 'a tissue of truth and fiction impossible to be extricated, the interlacings shall be so delicate, the partitions perfectly invisible.' And, in 'The Old Benchers of the Inner Temple', Elia says: 'let no one receive the narratives of Elia for true records. They are, in truth, but shadows of fact – verisimilitudes, not verities – or sitting but upon the remote edges and outskirts of history.' Elia was not Charles Lamb, Bridget was not Mary. Bridget was Mary's shadow – a shadow of a fact. A shadow may be inaccurate or exaggerated but it is not entirely a fallacy. It does tell us something about the object shadowed; for example, it gives a good idea of its shape and a sense of its volume. More significantly, a shadow changes according to the time of day it is seen and the angle from which it is seen. In Bridget, we have Mary seen by the man who knew her best and who loved her most, seen also at a particular time in Charles's life. He had reached maturity, given up – with regret but still finally – a dream of love and marriage and he was, at last, doing his best work. The Charles who created Bridget was not the despairing twenty-one-year-old who wished Mary dead. It was the Charles who had come to terms with his life and who could fully appreciate the rich and vital relationship that he enjoyed with his sister.

Bridget was born, fully formed, in February 1821 in the essay 'Mrs Battle's Opinions on Whist'. Charles's many nights spent among card players had not been wasted. His old friend Captain Burney's wife Sarah served as a model for Mrs Battle, a tough, take-no-prisoners player who 'loved a thorough-paced partner, a determined enemy', and regarded whist as 'her noble occupation . . . her business, her duty, the thing she came into the world to do – and she did it'. Mrs Battle would only play cards for money, maintaining that, without a stake, the game lacked its purpose, which was to make the skirmishes seem real. 'Cards are a temporary illusion; in truth, a mere drama; for we do but *play* at being mightily concerned, where a few idle shillings are at stake, yet, during the illusion, we *are* as mightily concerned as those whose stake is crowns or kingdoms.'

Bridget was the gentle counterpart to that Boudicca of the card table. And Elia has played cards 'for love' with his cousin Bridget. With a typically Elian mixture of the sensitive and the prosaic, the tender and the mundane, he wrote of playing whist with his 'sweet cousin' while waiting for her to apply a poultice to his foot. He evoked the domestic scene thus: 'I wished it might have lasted for ever, though we gained nothing, and lost nothing, thought it was a mere shade of play; I would be content to go on in that idle folly for ever. The pipkin should be ever boiling, that was to prepare the gentle lenitive to my foot, which Bridget was doomed to apply after the game was over; and as I do not much relish appliances, there it should ever bubble. Bridget and I should be ever playing.'

There was much suffering in the lives of Mary and Charles, a great deal of hardship, an overwhelming amount of pain, but there was also joy and playfulness. Charles Lamb celebrated that joy in the creation of Bridget. As Elia and Bridget, the brother and sister were transported into a sunnier world, a place where love ruled and 'idle folly' held sway. Years earlier, Charles had realised how easy it could be to forget to tell someone how you felt about them, to give in to a 'sort of indifference in the expression of kindness for each other' and had dedicated his first volume of poetry to Mary. Through the

Elia essays, he more than made up for any indifference there may have been.

In 'Mackery End', published in July 1821, Bridget appeared again. 'Bridget Elia has been my housekeeper for many a long year,' wrote Charles, 'I have obligations to Bridget, extending beyond the period of memory. We house together, old bachelor and maid, in a sort of double singleness.' They live together so comfortably that he feels more than adequately compensated for the lack of a wife. 'I, for one, find in myself no sort of disposition to go out upon the mountains, with the rash king's offspring, to bewail my celibacy,' he wrote.

'We are generally in harmony, with occasional bickerings as it should be among near relations. Our sympathies are rather understood than expressed; and once, upon my dissembling a tone in my voice more kind than ordinary, my cousin burst into tears, and complained that I was altered.'

In her tastes, Bridget was modern,

While I am hanging over (for the thousandth time) some passages in old Burton, or one of his strange contemporaries, she is abstracted in some modern tale, or adventure, whereof our common reading-table is daily fed with assiduously fresh supplies. Narrative teases me. I have little concern in the progress of events. She must have a story – well, ill, or indifferently, told – so there be life stirring in it, and plenty of good or evil accidents. The fluctuations of fortune in fiction, and almost in real life, have ceased to interest or operate but dully upon me. Out-of-the-way humours and opinions – heads with some diverting twist in them – the oddities of authorship please me most.

Practical Bridget 'has a native disrelish of anything that sounds odd or bizarre. Nothing goes down with her, that is

quaint, irregular, or out of the road of common sympathy.'
She 'holds nature more clever'.

Secure in her beliefs, although she has associated with 'free-thinkers – leaders and disciples, of novel philosophies and systems', none of them has ever had an effect on her views. 'That which was good and venerable to her, when a child, retains its authority over her mind still.' She was a good woman, a sound ethical compass to steer one's life by. 'Where we have differed upon moral points; upon something proper to be done, or let alone; whatever heat of opposition, or steadiness of conviction, I set out with, I am sure always, in the long run, to be brought over to her way of thinking.'

And, above all, she was fun to be with. 'She is excellent to be at a play with, or upon a visit; but best, when she goes on a journey with you.' The trip to Mackery End that had made Mary so happy is again recalled in this essay. Bridget's boldness in going into the old house, her joy at recognising and being recognised were all echoes of the feelings Mary had described in her letter. Mackery End and their experiences there were key to the Lambs' relationship. Charles was in Mary's charge then – 'her tender charge' – and, despite her madness and his responsibility for her madness, nothing had changed in essentials. Elia wrote that he was still Bridget's 'care in foolish manhood'.

These two essays were like love letters, prose poems in praise of a kind and loving woman. Bridget was Mary minus madness, a sunny, balanced, good-natured, secure individual who played and soothed and comforted. It was a Mary who knew her own mind, not the Mary who lost hers. Bridget was, for Charles, the essential Mary.

Three months after the publication of 'Mackery End', Mary fell ill again and, shortly afterwards, her brother John died. Her insanity on this occasion was a blessing, thought Charles;

for once he was 'in no hurry for her to recover, that the idea might be in her mind as long as it can, before she is able to comprehend its weight'. John Lamb left all his money and his pictures to his brother. Charles was moved to give John an even better legacy and immortalised him in the form of Elia's cousin James in the essay 'Dream Children'. There, the selfish, self-centred, rude John Lamb became a thorough hero, a splendid older brother to admire and look up to. He was 'so handsome and spirited a youth, and a king to the rest of us, and instead of moping about in solitary corners, like some of us, he would mount the most mettlesome horse he could get'. Grief softened Charles's criticism of his brother and made him into the much more likeable James.

Against this background of sorrow, young Emma Isola was like a bright light. She became like another member of the family and they were both proud and fond of her. Mary introduced her to another young girl, Victoria Novello, and endeared herself to them both by letting them slip away from the grown-ups and chat together in her bedroom. She organised a little dinner for them – roast chicken and a custard pudding and told them to eat up: 'Now remember, we all pick our bones. It isn't considered vulgar here to pick our bones.'

Charles took on the responsibility of Emma's education and paid for her to attend a boarding school in Dulwich kept by a Mrs Richardson and, after the death of her father, the little orphan began to spend more of her holidays with them in London. They taught her Latin and French and Emma's education may well have been in the their minds when they decided to embark on their most ambitious holiday to date – a trip to Paris. Charles was forty-seven, Mary was fifty-eight, any upheaval was likely to make Mary ill, so this was asking for trouble; neither of them had ever left the country, neither was confident in French, but they were determined to go.

The plan was to stay with their old theatre friend James Kenney who had married a Frenchwoman and now lived with his family at Versailles. According to Henry Crabb Robinson, Charles was in high spirits, Mary nervous. 'Her courage in going is great.' They prepared as well as they could, taking Mary's nurse, Miss James, and also a Frenchman – Guichet – to help with the practicalities. Sarah James was the daughter of a Shropshire rector and had once been employed as a nurse at Whitmore House asylum. She was now in private practice and, in that capacity, had started looking after Mary from about 1815. Perhaps in response to the Parliamentary Select Committee's shocking report into London's asylums, Charles had arranged for Mary to be treated at home rather than from home. They had enough rooms and Charles earned enough money to make that possible. Sarah James charged about 28 shillings a week and was given her board, except for her beer and her washing.

Mary was right to be nervous about the journey. At Amiens, she became ill and her holiday was brought to a halt while she recovered there, under the care of Miss James. Charles left her and went on to Paris taking the French guide with him. Neither Charles nor Mary left their account of that illness but it must have been terrifying for both of them. Mary Shelley, the poet's widow, had the story from the Kenneys. 'At Amiens, poor Miss L. was taken ill in her usual way, and Lamb was in despair. He met, however, with some acquaintances, who got Miss L. into proper hands, and L. came on to Versailles, and stayed with the Kenneys, going on very well, if the French wine had not been too good for him.'

The Lambs had planned to see Paris together and return home on the same boat. But because of Mary's illness Charles went back to London before her and, after her recovery, which was quick this time, she too went to stay with the Kenneys. Here she found a large, jolly family squeezed into a tiny house but there was always room for friends. Those few weeks were unique. For the first time since childhood, Mary was on holiday without her brother, for the first time in years they were apart and she was sane. He wrote her a letter from London – the only correspondence between the pair that exists – advising her of the best sights: 'You must walk all along the Borough side of the Seine facing the Tuileries. There is a mile and a half of print shops and book stalls. If the latter were but English. Then there is a place where the Paris people put all their dead people and bring them flowers and dolls and ginger bread nuts and sonnets and such trifles. And that is all I think worth seeing as sights, except that the streets and shops of Paris are themselves the best sight.'

The wonder was that Mary, after such a disastrous and frightening start to her holiday, could enjoy herself at all. But by now Mary was an old hand at relapse and recovery. She knew herself and her illness and, once she was better, she snatched at fun while she could. She had a high old time, getting on well with the Kenney family in Versailles and spending a week in Paris with Mrs Kenney. The family liked her; according to Mary Shelley, Kenney thought Mary Lamb was 'a faultless creature – possessing every virtue under heaven'. Henry Crabb Robinson arrived from London in August and spent a week squiring Mary and Mrs Kenney about Paris. With her friends, Mary walked and walked until she was tired. They looked at the pictures in the Louvre, wandered through the Palais Royal, visited the Panthéon and admired the flowers in the Jardin des Plantes and the Tuileries. They ate out at restaurants and snacked on ice cream at Tortoni's and spent evenings in the Café des Nymphes which Henry Crabb Robinson described as 'a low coffee house'. They were flâneurs in a city that has always been perfect for flâneurs. Wandering off the usual tourist tracks, they visited Paris's rag fair and Mary enjoyed it as much as the famous sights. They crossed and re-crossed the river Seine and walked past the site of the Bastille and walked up hills to get better views of the city. 'Oh the dear long dreary Boulevards! How I do wish to be just now stepping out of a Cuckoo into them!' Mary rhapsodised to Mrs James Kenney on her return to London.

She arrived back in September, having failed to smuggle a French waistcoat home for Crabb Robinson. She was happy but exhausted, at first too weak even to hold a pen. Charles wrote to the Kenneys on her behalf. When she felt better – it was not until two months later – she wrote an affectionate letter to Mrs Kenney. 'My thoughts are often with you, and your children's dear faces are perpetually before me. Give them all one additional kiss every morning for me. Remember there's one for Louisa, one to Ellen, one to Betsy, one to Sophia, one to James, one to Teresa, one to Virginia and one to Charles. Bless them all.' She was also embarrassed; no one could relish being known as the 'poor woman who went mad in a diligence on the way to Paris' as Mary Shelley described her. Mixed with her gratitude to Mrs Kenney, there is distress and shame. 'Thank you a thousand times for all your kindness to me. I know you will make light of the trouble my illness gave you; but the recollection of it often sits heavy on my heart. If I could ensure my health, how happy should I be to spend a month with you every summer.' However, the one thing she *couldn't* guarantee was her health and although once they were reunited back home Mary and Charles appeared to take up the pattern of their lives once more, the trip to Paris had shaken them more than they realised and had finally convinced them that city life with its excitement was too much for them. Miss James needed to be with Mary frequently. Charles wrote his farewell to their old way of life in the Elia essay 'Old China', giving Bridget a monologue – more than 1,500 words long – in which she muses on and mourns the happy days when they were poorer. 'I wish the good old times would come again,' says Bridget, 'when we were not quite so rich.' She does not want to be poor exactly, just poor enough to make cheap luxuries – old folios, prints, picnic lunches, one-shilling gallery seats at the theatre, strawberries, new peas – seem like events, as in days of their former, relative poverty. Now, says Bridget, 'a purchase is but a purchase, now that you have money enough and to spare. Formerly it used to be a triumph.' Elia listens sympathetically – 'Bridget is so sparing of her speech on most occasions, that when she gets into a rhetorical vein, I am careful how I interrupt it' – but he reminds her that 'it is true we were happier when we were poorer, but we were also younger'. Charles and Mary had both realised that an era in their lives was coming to an end and, in this, one of the most charmingly detailed and nostalgic Elia essays, he gave his sister more than a half share in the expression of regret and goodbye.

In September 1823, they finally made the change they had been thinking about, discussing and experimenting with for years – they moved out of London, leaving their rooms in bustling Covent Garden for a home in the nearby village of Islington. Their new home was a white cottage, the first house they had ever lived in; until then they had always lived in rooms and apartments. The rooms were cheerful and light and, filled with their books, soon looked comfortable and familiar. Friends of the Lambs were puzzled by such an extreme relocation. Leigh Hunt even wrote an article for the *Examiner* on their defection from the metropolis. 'Why didst thou leave the warm crowd of humanity, which thou lovest so well, to go and shiver on the side of the New River, enticing thy unwary friends to walk in? Were friends and sitting up at night too attractive? And was there no other way to get rid of them?'

For a while, Charles wrote enthusiastically about being, finally, a householder and he waxed lyrical about gardening – 'quite a new sort of occupation to me . . . I do now sit under my own vine and contemplate the growth of vegetable nature. I can now understand in what sense they speak of FATHER ADAM.' It was a large garden, full of pears, strawberries, parsnips, leeks, carrots and cabbages, and at the end of it ran the sluggish, now vanished New River. The move, though made with Mary's long-term health in mind, had its usual effect in the short term and she was so ill this time she needed to go to an asylum. She returned a couple of months later but didn't seem much better; for several months, there was silence from her while Charles wrote letters on her behalf. The change from Londoners to countryfolk was hard for both of them. However much he joked about being 'lord (for the first time) of a dunghill', the truth was they both felt out of their element. For Mary, who did not even have the distraction of daily work, the new house – and new way of life – must have come particularly hard. It was not that their friends ignored them: many made the trip to Islington, George Dyer came to call and absentmindedly walked into the New River. A panic-stricken Mary gasped, 'Poor Mr Dyer', but rose to the occasion and put him to bed with a brandy and water. Their friend, Thomas Hood, a sub-editor at the *London Magazine*, lived nearby and spent at least three evenings week at their cottage but, even with that and setting aside the sort of occasional drama that George Dyer brought, Colebrook Row was dull compared with Covent Garden. Neither Mary nor Charles relished the feeling of no longer being at the centre of things.

In these circumstances, Emma Isola became an increasingly important part of their lives. She was young, healthy, good-natured – Henry Crabb Robinson said that 'as a girl she was beautiful' – and, most importantly, she was at the very start of her life. Her presence helped turn their focus away from their own miserable health and their own intense, claustrophobic relationship. When Emma's father had died in 1823, the Lambs had assumed a more complete responsibility for her and, from then on, her home in the school holidays became their home. It was a bold move, a daring bid for a new kind of family life. Old maid and old bachelor they might be, but they were still able, by taking care of Emma, to experience some of the pleasures of, if not parenthood, then at least guardianship. There were many risks attached. Even though Emma was away a great deal, they were still introducing another person into that 'atmosphere of sad mental uncertainty' that the older, wiser, more socially assured and self-determining Fanny Kelly had rejected. If Emma was living with them, there could be no hiding Mary's breakdowns from Emma. However, they did try to hide from her the fact that Mary had killed her mother. Years later, an edition of Charles Lamb's works described how: '. . . during the whole period of her residence with the Lambs she was completely ignorant of the terrible event. One night, Charles and Mary Lamb and herself were seated at table. The conversation turned on the elder Lamb, when Miss Isola asked why she never heard mention of the mother. Mary thereupon uttered a sharp, piercing cry, for which Charles playfully and laughingly rebuked her, but he made no allusion to the cause.'

The need for silence, the wondering if anyone else had let

the story slip must have been stressful. Yet the Lambs were often uncommunicative even with each other on issues that were important to them. In 1824, they made a further break with habit and didn't take their usual summer holiday – Charles was hoping staying at home would be good for Mary but he had not mentioned that hope to her. He wrote, in a letter to William Wordsworth, 'Mary is in capital health, and I have a hope at bottom, that it be better for her, that we did not go out of town this summer. I have a conceit, that she has one, that she may escape illness by this moderation. Her thinking so (though we say nothing about it) may go a great way.' They were close but it was not always the closeness where every thought was shared and every decision debated together. Sometimes they preferred to assume or intuit each other's feelings; some thoughts were best left unexpressed. For a while, the plan of living quietly seemed to be working. Mary had no attack in 1824, the first year she had been free of illness since 1819.

Charles longed for his own freedom; he was, he said, 'ominously tired of official confinement'. The possibility of early retirement from the East India Company was uppermost in his mind. He consulted Mary's old doctor, Dr Tuthill, who wrote a letter on his behalf to the company, explaining his ill health. In February 1825, Charles officially requested to be allowed to retire. He was kept in suspense for a couple of months and then in March, shortly after his fiftieth birthday, he was given his freedom 'on account of certified ill health'. After thirty-three years, he left his desk with a pension of £450 a year. He was overjoyed. 'I have left the d—d India Office for ever,' he wrote to Henry Crabb Robinson, and to another friend he rejoiced, 'I am free – free as air.' He called his retirement his 'gaol delivery' and was almost dizzy with excitement. He was 'staggered . . . confused . . . giddy . . .'. Once he calmed down, he felt 'a degree or two above content'. Mary, he said, 'wakes every morning with an obscure feeling that some good has happened to us'. There was, however, a problem – to be faced by Mary as well as himself – what on earth was he to do with all that time?

Charles and Mary.

Chapter 13

A Very Sorry Pair of Phenomena

*O let no native Londoner imagine that health, and
rest, and innocent occupation, interchange of converse
sweet and recreative study, can make the country any
thing better than altogether odious and detestable*
Charles Lamb, letter to
William Wordsworth, 1830

LIKE MANY A DESK-BOUND wage slave, Charles had dreamed
of freedom. Once liberated, he found that his work routine
had been a useful crutch as well as a straitjacket. He and Mary
had already removed themselves from their familiar haunts,
now they were to lose their familiar routine and, without those
structures, the whole edifice of their lives began to look shaky.
In April, he was rejoicing and talking of going travelling with
Mary; in May, he wrote his Elia essay 'The Superannuated
Man', tracing the emotional arc of the retired man from 'giddy
raptures' through missing his 'old chains' to appreciation of
'the life contemplative'. However, in reality, he was beginning
to feel that excessive leisure could be a burden. By mid-summer
he was mentally ill – an 'attack on his nerves', Crabb Robinson
called it – and by September he had experienced a full-scale
nervous breakdown. He was irritable, depressed, insomniac,

unable to bear company. 'I am very feeble,' he wrote to a friend, 'can scarce move a pen.' He wrote sad scraps of letters to his friends. For years he had dreaded and resisted mental illness – 'the sorest malady of all' – and now here he was, mentally disabled. Mary worried over him until she broke down herself. Charles was convinced that she would be 'deprived of reason for many weeks to come'. He had daily visits from a doctor and Miss James moved in to take care of Mary. Brother and sister were still living together but they were essentially separated, their daily lives running in different grooves. They were both ill, both unhappy and neither could do a thing to help the other. The house, said Charles with considerable under-statement, was 'gloomy'. It was not until December that the Lambs felt well enough to receive visitors again.

They had been miserable when they were ill and apart; their intense closeness was very apparent afterwards, reinforced by all the time they were spending together now that Charles had retired. The journalist Peter Patmore, who became friends with Charles around this time, said that 'all their personal thoughts, feelings, and associations were so entirely centred in those of each other, that it was only by an almost painful effort they were allowed to wander elsewhere, even at the brief intervals claimed by that social intercourse which they nevertheless could not persuade themselves wholly to shun. They had been for so many years accustomed to look to each other alone for sympathy and support that they could scarcely believe these to exist apart from themselves. This gave to both an absent and embarrassed air.' Mrs Balmanno, who met them at Hood's house the following year, was struck by the way Mary's eyes rarely left her brother's face, recalling: 'Even when apparently engrossed in conversation with others, she (Mary) would by supplying some word for which he was at a loss, even when talking in a distant part of the room show how clearly her mind waited upon his.' Charles, she noted, surrounded his sister with 'instances of affection and evidences of ever watchful solitude'. He also, she remarked, teased her constantly. Mary's saint-like good humour and patience were as remarkable as his strange and whimsical modes of trying them. He would jump up suddenly, clap her on the shoulder and shout: 'I had a sister, the devil kissed her and raised a blister.' He turned familiarity and formality topsy-turvy, joking that he called his sister Maria when they were alone, Mary when they were with friends and Moll before the servants. According to Mary Balmanno, Charles was full of 'pranks and oddities' towards her and sometimes he sounded so rude that listeners were startled. Mary, though, took it all in her stride, understanding that his outbursts were the outpouring of an affection that needed expression but which disliked to parade itself too obviously in public. Just as Elia had been the perfect cover for some of Charles's deepest feelings – 'I retire, impenetrable to ridicule, under the phantom-cloud of Elia,' he once wrote – so he teased his sister to disguise how much he cared for her and how much he needed her. Once, when he'd gone too far, shocking his visitors with his rudeness, he dropped his jokes for a few days until Mary, in tears, asked if he was angry with her.

However, his drinking did worry her. Patmore recalled that Charles 'would never let you go away from his house, whatever might be the weather or the hour, without walking several miles with you on your road. And his talk was always more free and flowing on these occasions. There was, however, another reason for these walks. In whatever direction they lay, Lamb always saw at the end of them the pleasant vision of a foaming pot of porter . . . When Lamb was quitting home with you to accompany you part of the way on your journey, you could always see that his sister had rather he stayed at home; and not seldom her last salutation to him on his leaving the

room was – "Now, you're not going to drink any ale, Charles?"
"No! No!" was his half impatient reply.'

When they were well, much of their happiness came from taking care of Emma; she became a sort of joint project for the Lambs as they set about preparing her to be a governess, remaking her in their own bookish mould. Mary continued teaching her French, Charles was responsible for improving her arithmetic and they both taught her Latin. Essentially, they gave her the kind of education that Mary would have enjoyed and benefited from as a young girl. Emma, on the other hand, was no bluestocking and found her lessons a struggle. She was, according to Mary, 'sadly deficient' in arithmetic and she found Latin a painful chore. Mary wrote her an affectionate sonnet – 'To Emma Learning Latin and Desponding' – when she was downcast by her declensions.

Droop not, dear Emma, dry those falling tears,
And call up smiles into thy pallid face,
Pallid and care-worn with thy arduous race:
In few brief months thou hast done the work of years.
To young beginnings natural are those fears.
A right good scholar shalt thou one day be,
And that no distant one; when even she,
Who now to thee a star far off appears,
That most rare Latinist, the Northern Maid –
The language-loving Sarah of the Lake –
Shall hail thee Sister Linguist. This will make
Thy friends, who now afford thee careful aid,
A recompense most rich for all their pains,
Counting thy acquisitions their best gains.

Emma's presence changed Mary's relationship with Charles.
When Mary was ill, it was Emma who went out with Charles

in the evenings. The young girl replaced Mary in many of his long walks, her young legs managing to keep up; as Mary's bouts of illness got longer and longer and her once excellent physical health was undermined by old age, Emma became Charles's 'only walk-companion'. He took her to see Coleridge, now living in Highgate on a modified opium regime under the permanent care of a doctor. There, she pleased both Coleridge and Lamb by reading aloud 'some of the most difficult passages in the *Paradise Lost*' in a 'very excellent manner'. She 'teased' Charles to take her to the opera and he obliged. He wrote joint letters with her, as he had always done with Mary. Henry Crabb Robinson described him as being 'quite eloquent in praise of Miss Isola; he says she is the most sensible girl, and the best female talker he knows. He wants to see her well married, great as the loss would be to him.' Just as Fanny had, Emma awoke the poet in Charles; he praised her character and mind in verse.

> External gifts of fortune, or of face,
> Maiden, in truth, thou hast not much to show;
> Much fairer damsels have I known, and know,
> And richer may be found in every place.

> In thy *mind* seek thy beauty, and thy wealth.
> Sincereness lodgeth there, the soul's best health.
> O guard that treasure above gold or pear,
> Laid up secure from moths and worldly stealth –
> And take my benison, plain-hearted girl.

He called her 'our nut-brown maid' and 'a girl of gold'. When she went away, to visit her aunt or other friends, he spoke openly about how much he missed her. Her going was an 'unhinging time'.

Mary worked hard to find a governess position for Emma, writing to Lady Stoddart, her old friend Sarah's sister-in-law. 'I am moving heaven and earth, that is to say, I am pressing the matter upon all the very few friends I have that are likely to assist me in such a case, to get her into a family as a governess.' As well as trying to find a post for Emma, Charles also put himself out to garner contributions from his literary friends that Emma could include in her album. There was, at the time, a trend among young women for this sort of activity, collecting together a miscellany of poems, acrostics and quotations – Jane Austen used the young lady's album to great effect in *Emma* where acrostics are employed to confuse and muddle the heroine, her protégée, Harriet Smith and the looking-out-for-a-wife clergyman, Mr Elton. In verse, Charles dismissed albums as being '. . . a book kept by modern young ladies for show, / Of which their plain grandmothers nothing did know. A medley of scraps, half verse, and half prose, / And some things not very like either, God knows.' Yet he took up Emma's with enthusiasm. He called it 'a superb "forget me not" sort of thing' and he asked, among others, Bryan Proctor and Walter Savage Landor. He thanked his friends profusely but was aware that he was making himself look foolish. He begged some lines of verse from Bryan Proctor and admitted 'by dabbling in those accursed Albums, I have become a byword of infamy all over the kingdom'. He found the album form irresistible though, writing all manner of acrostics and finally having his *Album Verses* – a collection of light verse and acrostics – published. Many of the poems mentioned Emma Isola.

Mary was fond of Emma, speaking of her visits with pleasure, but there is no record of her immersing herself in the young girl and her concerns to the extent that Charles did. She called her simply Emma while Charles adopted the more intimate amusement of playing word games with her name. Verses for her album are 'adopted into the splendid Emmatic constellation'. When the young girl tries her hand at poetry, he says they are not 'lyrics or heroics but Emmaics'. Puns and wordplay were always more Charles's style than Mary's but her letters to Sarah Stoddart show that she too could be humorous and playful where she was exceptionally fond. Her tone in speaking of Emma is affectionate but practical. She wrote of her accomplishments and was enthusiastic and energetic in finding her a place. But although Charles referred to the girl as 'our young friend', she seems to have been mainly *his* young friend. Emma called him her 'dear friend', but had no special term for Mary.

Charles was still restless, unsure what to with his time in retirement, seeking out change for change's sake. Patmore thought he was never 'wholly at his ease for half an hour together – wholly free from that restlessness which is incompatible with mental tranquillity'. In September 1827, Charles moved house again, transporting Mary and Emma to Enfield, a small village still further away from the heart of London. He thought the countryside around was beautiful and he praised the new house as 'most compact and desirable'. On their first evening there, Mary looked round it, pronounced 'how frightfully like this room is to our room in Islington', and almost instantly became mad. Moving was, once again, too much for her. She didn't go to an asylum; instead she lived in isolation in their new house, looked after by Miss James. Visitors were banned because even a knock at the door made her worse. Her illness lasted for eleven weeks and Charles missed her but, on this occasion, his letters on the subject of her illness were calmer. He was sure that she would recover – 'she always comes round again', he wrote almost breezily – and he had Emma and her Latin lessons to distract him. When his young friend left for a post of governess in Suffolk, her departure left 'an ugly gap'.

Did Charles love Emma? Should we read his energy around her rather silly album as the action of an admirer or an affectionate father-figure? He cared deeply for her, he enjoyed her company, made himself responsible for her welfare. For her sake, he began to change the way in which Mary's illnesses were managed. When she was ill in May 1829 and Emma and an old schoolfriend were due for a holiday, instead of Miss James and her own bedroom, Mary was sent away to an asylum in Fulham, owned by Talfourd's parents. The two young girls came to stay in her absence and his loneliness was 'a little abated'. He felt that he was losing Mary, she was ill so often and for longer and longer stretches of time – three months was now the usual period of illness. In her depression, she was 'scarce showing any pleasure in seeing me or curiosity when I should come again'. Emma was his comfort. When he was depressed – which was frequently – she was one of the few people he was happy to see. In her company, he was on his best behaviour; for her sake, he made efforts to keep his drinking under control, at least when they were in other people's houses. Mary came home from Fulham, still ill – 'low spirited and utterly unable to manage', wrote Charles. Mary was now sixty-four years old, frequently rheumatic, suffered badly with toothache, was short-sighted and, every year, lost almost three months of her life to madness. She was no longer capable of running his household and their 'old petted servant' Becky was leaving them to get married which put them 'in a fidget'. Crabb Robinson always said that Becky was 'ill-tempered' and had 'been a plague and a tyrant to them' but she was a familiar plague and tyrant. She had been with them for so long she was part of the family. Stressed, as ever, by change, Mary was 'frightened at the idea of a *new* servant'. In September, while Mary was still 'in the saddest low spirits that ever poor crea-ture had', Charles, in a burst of nervous impetuosity, sold all their furniture and moved himself and Mary into lodgings in the house next door. 'Mary's bad spirits drove me upon it,' he said. At one stroke, they lost the 'cares of housekeeping' but they also lost their independence. Their landlords, the Westwoods were, said Charles, 'an honest couple' but the move from householders to lodgers was not easy. They took their meals with the Westwoods but they had nothing in common with them; Westwood, before his retirement to Enfield, had been a haberdasher. For a while, Mary thrived under the new arrangement; she told Dorothy Wordsworth that she found it 'very quiet and comfortable' and Charles said the move had 'the most beneficial effects' on her. 'She looks two years and a half younger for it', he maintained. But he hated it; he fretted 'like a lion in a net'. However hard he tried, he could never accustom himself to the countryside. 'What have I gained by health?' he moaned. 'Intolerable dullness. What by early hours and moderate meals? – a total blank.'

Mary made friends with the Westwoods' young son, Thomas, teaching him Latin and sharing her love of novels with him. He remembered how she was sent 'huge parcels of modern novels' that she was allowed to read but not keep or cut open. The old lady and the young boy looked at them together. 'Excellent Bridget Elia!' wrote Thomas, confusing, as others did, the woman with the character. 'She was a good Latinist and a great devourer of novels, and I am proud to avow that my first knowledge of Latin and first taste for fiction both came from her.' Mary and Charles still enjoyed their game of whist but cards were no longer the thrill they had been in the good old days in Inner Temple Lane; now they were just a way of making the evenings pass quicker. Enfield was dreary. There was plenty of countryside for the Lambs to walk in – Mary might have been slowing up but, at sixty-five, she could still manage her twelve hours a day – and they had plenty of visitors but there were no theatres, no stalls selling old books and prints, no circulating libraries. A reasonably sized village, Enfield lacked the dramatic wildness of real countryside but also the anonymity of city streets. Mary and Charles had been uprooted from everything they knew and loved best and the effect on them was not good. In particular, it drove Charles to drink.

The following year, it was Emma who was ill; she had brain fever (cerebrospinal meningitis) and the Lambs were frantic with worry. Charles wrote a desperate letter to Emma's employer, Mrs Williams. He and his sister were 'in great distress'; he begged to be told 'from day to day, the state she is in'. When the news came that she was on the mend, Mary cried with relief. Charles left her alone and went to bring Emma home to recuperate. Once she had fully recovered, he wrote a poem to her:

> Had I but gold to my desire,
> You still should walk in silk attire;
> If I had health, and if health were
> Transferable as riches are,
> I'd give you, Emma, half of mine.

The wealth, the health, the giving – the lines hinted at the words of the marriage service but the bestowal is conditional – *if* he had these things and then only half. Perhaps he was only half in love. In another poem, 'To a Child of Quality', he wrote as if he were alive to the impossibility – and therefore the possibility – of romantic and sexual love between them.

> For, as our different ages move,
> 'tis so ordain'd – would fate but mend it! –
> That I shall be past making love,
> When she begins to comprehend it.

She was too young, he too old and he had assumed the fatherly role in her life. It would have been a match as unsuitable as the one he described in the poem he was writing at that time, a hilarious verse called 'Satan in Search of a Wife'. And, even if none of those things had been true, there was always Mary and Mary's devil. Yet in these, the last years of his life, Emma touched something in him. She brought out in him, just as Fanny Kelly had done, tenderness and a vein of loving chivalry but, unlike Fanny, Emma was dependent enough and youthful enough to appreciate it. Mary felt it. Years later, speaking in one of her manic moments, she told Henry Crabb Robinson that her brother and Emma had been in love with each other. Crabb Robinson dismissed the claim as 'utterly wild and groundless', and put it down to the fact that Mary was not in her right mind at the time. But not all the utterances of the mad are incorrect, and perhaps she had seen into Charles's heart in a way that even such an old friend as Crabb Robinson could not. The young woman's presence in their lives was a blessing for both of them but there was, unmistakeably, a great deal of tension in the Lamb household during the years she lived there too. They were all suffering, twisting about, trying to get comfortable, to settle themselves.

For a brief period in 1830, Mary and Charles tried living in rooms back in London, in what had been one of their earliest homes, Southampton Buildings, but the experiment was a failure. After recovering from her brain fever, Emma too became ill with what sounds like a nervous breakdown and was dismissed by her employers. Mary was very ill that year, throughout the autumn and winter. She was 'in a deplorable state' said Charles. 'I almost fear whether she has strength at her time of life ever to get out of it.' This time, she was nursed at home – the Fulham experiment was not repeated – but she stayed in her bedroom, made worse by the slightest agitation.

Even to read or write a letter in front of her made her upset. Charles lost his bearings and drank even more than normal. He got so drunk at Bryan Proctor's house one night that he couldn't stand up and Martin Burney had to carry him out of the room. A visit to Henry Crabb Robinson in October 1831 saw him starting on the brandy at nine o'clock in the morning. Robinson said he was always 'tipsy and thoroughly uncomfortable' and worried that he was bringing 'destruction' on himself. Sometimes he was so drunk he couldn't walk. He worried his friends and disgusted people who did not know him – 'a confirmed, shameless drunkard' was the verdict of the acerbic Thomas Carlyle. He thought Lamb was 'in some considerable degree, insane' and he noted, with deep disapproval, how Lamb 'asks vehemently for gin and water in strangers' houses, tipples till he is utterly mad, and is only not thrown out of doors because he is too much despised for taking such trouble with him'. He thought that Charles and Mary were 'a very sorry pair of phenomena'.

For those who loved them they were objects of pity. Mary was so ill, so often and so severely that even their boarding house arrangement was no longer working. They no longer liked the Westwoods, their landlords; Charles called them 'detestable'. He felt the Westwoods were taking advantage; there was no longer a Becky to make sure the unworldly Lambs were not exploited. Patmore recalled that, although the Lambs paid 'a price, almost sufficient to keep all the household twice over, but where, nevertheless, they were expected to pay for every extra cup of tea, or any other refreshment, they might offer to any occasional visitor'. They were charged an extra sixpence when Wordsworth visited because the poet, said the Westwoods, 'had taken such a quantity of sugar in his tea'. Also, Mr Westwood was old and seemed to be getting senile. The situation was grim and horribly like the bad days in Little

Queen Street, where constricted living and general illness had worked its terrible effect on Mary. When the whole household went down with flu and Mary recovered from it only to become mad again, it was clear she needed better care.

A few miles away in Edmonton, Charles found the Waldens. Mr Walden had been a keeper at a mental asylum and now let out rooms in his house to patients. Locals remembered that the Waldens 'made their living by keeping in gentle restraint those whose attacks were harmless or intermittent, and whose friends looked for more humane treatment that was obtainable in the asylums'. Charles decided to place Mary under Mr Walden's care and to live in the house himself. It might have seemed like a supreme act of charity for him to confine himself to the restrictions of a lunatic asylum but, as he told a friend of Emma's, he could be 'nowhere happier than under the same roof' as Mary. Moreover, his own behaviour was so odd by this time that, according to one neighbour, 'the reputation of insanity' was associated with 'the brother as well as the sister'. Emma too would have to make her home behind the small cottage's high iron gates. It was not a style of living anyone, let alone a young woman of twenty-four, would relish.

Emma's marriage came as a relief to all three of them. Her husband, Edward Moxon, was a poet and publisher who had published some of Charles's work. He had been showing an interest in Emma for some time and the couple married in 1833. Charles gave Emma money on her marriage and also a painting of Milton that had been left to him by his brother. He also gave her away; Mary was not at the wedding; she was one of the last to know that an engagement had taken place. She had been ill for some days but, the day after the wedding, she wrote a curious letter to Emma.

'My dear Emma and Edward Moxon,' she wrote. 'Accept my sincere congratulations, and imagine more good wishes than my weak nerves will let me put into good set words. The drear blank of unanswered questions which I ventured to ask in vain was cleared up on the wedding-day by Mrs W. taking a glass of wine, and with a total change of countenance, begged leave to drink Mr and Mrs Moxon's health. It restored me, from that moment: as if by an electrical stroke: to the entire possession of my senses – I never felt so calm and quiet after a similar illness as I do now. I feel as if all tears were wiped from my eyes and all care from my heart.'

None of her previous bouts of illness had ended this way and it is not at all the pattern of manic-depressive illness. It is tempting to see what happened here as a sort of sophisticated malingering. Mary clearly did suffer from a mental illness; the great battle of her life was to fight it. In that struggle to which she brought courage, determination and optimism, it is possible that she had learnt that there were occasions when it was worth making it work for her. She could not prevent her flights into mania or her descents into depression but perhaps she had some control over her return from them. And perhaps she did not choose to get better until after Emma's wedding. If that is the case, why didn't she want to go to Emma's wedding? Perhaps, as much as being Edward and Emma's day, it was also Charles and Emma's. He gave the bride away – 'was father at the wedding', as he put it. And, out of kindness to her brother and a sense of self-preservation in herself, she thought it best to be absent while he said his goodbyes to his 'nut-brown maid'.

Chapter 14

A Not Unpeaceful Evening

Love is the passion which endureth,
Which neither time nor absence cureth;
Which nought of earthly change can sever:
Love is the light which shines for ever.

What cold and selfish breasts deem madness
Lives in its depths of joy and sadness:
In hearts, on lips, of flame it burneth;
One is its world – to one it turneth.

Its chain of gold – what hand can break it?
Its deathless hold – what force can shake it?
Mere passion aught of earth may sever
But souls that love – love on for ever.
          'What is Love', Mary Lamb, *The Keepsake*, 1829

H E IS SEATED. SHE stands to his right and a little behind him. He could be an elderly cleric; she could almost be his mother. The years have brought him a receding hairline, pinched his always-thin cheeks and accentuated the length of his nose. She, with her short, square body and frilly white bonnet, could have stood as a model for Little Red Riding Hood's grandmother. But the hair under her frills is still dark

and full and the mouth is humorous. Both stare out of the canvas but at a slight angle, their bodies and faces turned inwards towards each other. They are painted in layers of darkness, their sombre clothes merging with the shadowy walls, their faces the brightest spots in the room. To Mary's right, light from an invisible source illuminates some paper and three quill pens standing in an inkpot, ready to hand.

Francis Stephen Cary painted Mary and Charles Lamb in 1834 and he caught them well. Their closeness, their old-fashioned dress, their eccentricity and, above all, their age – Mary is seventy, Charles fifty-nine – and both look weathered by time and experience. There is the reference to writing in the paper and inkpots.

By then they were persons of some celebrity. Lamb had something of a fan club; many admirers made the journey specifically to enjoy, and often record, a meeting with Elia. Nathaniel Parker Willis, an American journalist and poet, met Lamb and his sister in June 1834 and he too was struck by the appearance of Mary's age and illness. He described her as 'a small bent figure, evidently a victim to ill-health and hears with difficulty'. But he went on to say that 'her face has been, I should think, fine and handsome and her bright grey eye is still full of intelligence and fire'.

Charles still liked to tease her. Willis recalled how he was 'continually taking advantage of her deafness to mystify her with the most singular gravity upon every topic that was started'. He pretended that she not he was the author of the essay 'Confessions of a Drunkard'. After eating, Charles 'left the table and began to wander round the room with a broken, uncertain step, as if he almost forgot to put one leg before the other. His sister rose after a while, and commenced walking up and down very much in the same manner on the opposite side of the table'. It was strange behaviour though Willis loyally refused to term it so.

They were both still taking snuff and Charles was still drinking heavily. Another Lamb admirer and visitor to their home that year, a Reverend J. Fuller Russell, recalled their amiable bickering on the subject. When Lamb mixed himself some rum and water, 'His sister objected to this operation, and he refrained. Presently after he said, "May I have a little drop now, only a *leetle* drop?" "No, be a good boy." At last he prevailed and took his usual draught.'

Their new acquaintances were charmed by them but they caused great anxiety to the people who knew them well. The year of the Cary portrait – 1834 – had begun with Mary falling ill. She was insane and violent for almost twenty weeks, 'as bad as poor creature can be,' said Charles. And yet, even then, she was still the anchor to which he held. Her ravings, the ceaseless manic monologues that he 'too often' heard, were still the sounds he loved best. He told one of Emma's friends that, so long as she wasn't violent, he thought Mary's 'rambling chat' was better than 'the sense and sanity of this world'. Always nostalgic – the essays of Elia were a sustained exploration of nostalgia and reminiscence – he valued the way the intense activity of Mary's manic brain kept him in touch with their shared past. 'Her memory is unnaturally strong,' he wrote:

And from ages past, if we may so call the earliest records of our poor life, she fetches thousands of names and things that never would have dawned upon me again and thousands from the ten years she lived before me. What took place from early girlhood to her coming of age principally lives (every important thing and every trifle) in her brain with the vividness of real presence. For twelve hours incessantly she will pour out without intermission all her past life, forgetting nothing, pouring out name after name (to the Waldens) as a dream; sense and nonsense; truths and errors huddled together; a medley between inspiration and possession.

It was powerful, it was exhilarating, it was exhausting. Each episode of illness was worse than the one before. 'She has less and less strength to throw it off, and they leave a dreadful depression after them,' Charles wrote. Mary did her best to stay sane: she walked out with him, she looked forward to quiet enjoyments, she struggled to be happy. But she was losing the battle.

Then, in July, came news of their dear friend Coleridge's death. That, in addition to Mary's mania and melancholy, unhinged Charles still further. It was not that he saw Coleridge frequently but the bonds of their friendship had been tied tight, long ago, in their childhoods and, next to Mary, he was the person Charles loved best. Coleridge thought of Charles – and of his sister – on his deathbed, sending them both a mourning ring, and the words: 'To my close friend and ever-beloved schoolfellow, Charles Lamb – and in the deep and almost life-long affection of which this is the slender record; his equally-beloved sister, Mary Lamb, will know herself to be included.'

Charles couldn't get over the loss of his oldest friend. The historian and biographer John Forster wrote that 'he thought of little else . . . He had a habit of venting his melancholy in a sort of mirth... Some old friends of his saw him two or three weeks ago, and remarked the constant turning and reference of his mind. He interrupted himself and them almost every instant with some play of affected wonder, or astonishment, or humorous melancholy, on the words, "Coleridge is dead." Nothing could divert him from that, for the thought of it never left him.'

Death as well as madness had always been the Lambs' constant companion. Their domestic contentment had sprung out of their mother's death at Mary's hand, their life together began on the death of their father. Charles experienced Mary's absences as a sort of death. Not surprisingly, both sister and brother thought a lot about mortality. Some of Charles's best jokes were about fake deaths. He'd killed Mary off in sport – when his good friend Manning was due home from China in 1815, Charles had written: 'You must not expect to see the same England again which you left... Mary has been dead and buried many years – she desired to be buried in the silk gown you sent her.' He once sealed a letter to Vincent Novello with a black seal, explaining inside in a jokey postscript: 'I sign with a black seal, that you may begin to think her cold has killed Mary, which will be an agreeable unsurprise when you read the Note.' He and Mary talked together about their own deaths and were of the same mind. Charles Cowden Clarke recalls an incident – Lamb 'once said (with his peculiar mode of tenderness, beneath blunt, abrupt speech "you must die first, Mary." She nodded, with her little quiet nod, and sweet smile, "Yes, I must die first, Charles."'

Her decline was evident and her death expected. In November, Henry Crabb Robinson was writing of her that there was 'now no longer hope for any continued health, her case is now hopeless'. In the end though, and to everyone's surprise, it was Charles who died first.

On Monday 22 December 1834, he went out for a walk and fell, grazing his face. He may well have been drunk at the time. An infection set in and, by Friday, he had developed erysipelas. This disease, which these days can be successfully cured with antibiotics, can spread quickly. A general feeling of unwellness and headaches swiftly becomes nausea and high fever. A rash of itchy red patches spreads across the nose and cheeks. The spots become blisters that burst and then crust over. Untreated, the infection spreads to the brain. Talfourd saw Charles on Friday, Boxing Day, and reported to worried friends that he was most definitely 'in danger'. On Saturday morning, he was barely conscious; Talfourd found him 'weak, and nearly insensible to things passing around him'. He murmured the names of friends in a faint voice. Mary knew nothing about the drama unfolding in her own house. She was in her bedroom, out of her mind, aware of nothing but her own fantasies and demons. The fall, the illness, the doctors coming and going, if these things reached her they came as if from a distance, their significance dulled and rendered, for a while, meaningless. And she was mercifully, blissfully unaware of the moment when, later on that Saturday, her brother died. Death, which had stalked Mary for years, took Charles quickly.

For once Mary's devil was a friend, taking away her reason and blurring the pain that knowledge would have brought. Talfourd described her as being 'in a state of partial estrangement, which, while it did not wholly obscure her mind, deadened her feelings, so that as she gradually regained her perfect senses she felt as gradually the full force of the blow, and was the better able calmly to bear it'. She was taken to see her dead brother's body and exclaimed how beautiful he was. Despite being 'quite insane' in Crabb Robinson's words, she was still able to point out a spot for his grave – a quiet plot in the nearby churchyard in Edmonton, close to where she lived.

She was too ill to attend his funeral and she continued in that alienated state for some time. Crabb Robinson visited her a few weeks after her brother's death and found her 'neither violent nor unhappy, nor was she entirely without sense. She was however out of her mind, as the ordinary expression is.' She was delighted to see her old friend. 'Oh, here's Crabby,' she exclaimed delightedly and thanked him for coming before embarking on a chaotic anecdote. 'I am glad to see you, but don't you be teasing me about Mrs Anthony Robinson. She was a good woman, as good as ever breathed, but she behaved very ill to Mr Cresswell . . .' Henry Crabb Robinson listened to her running on and on about the 'unhappy insane family' of Anthony Robinson. 'It would be useless to attempt recollecting all she said, but it is to be remarked that her mind seemed turned to subjects connected with insanity as well as with her bother's death. She spoke of Charles repeatedly but not in a tone of the least sorrow.' But she still had enough of her wits about her to play a game of piquet with Crabb Robinson and to enjoy beating him.

She told him she was worried about money, offering to mend his stockings for a fee. It was probably one of the tasks she performed for Charles out of love. Actually, she was quite well off. Charles's will surprised everybody; his estate yielded £2,000 and the East India House later agreed to pay her a pension of £120 a year. Nobody expected him to leave so much – he had clearly been saving for years – and nobody expected that Mary would need the money for long. Her friends were convinced that, without her brother, Mary would soon die. Barron Field talked of 'Lamb's death and of Mary Lamb's death-in-life' and Crabb Robinson was sure that Charles's death 'must draw after it that of his admirable but wretched sister, who is now in a state of derangement and will probably recover only to hear of her irreparable loss and die.' Dorothy Wordsworth wrote that Mary still survived as 'a solitary twig – patiently enduring the storm of life. In losing her brother she lost her all – all but the remembrance of him, which cheers her the day through.' Edward Moxon expressed the same sense of Mary's desolation in verse:

> . . . she who comes each evening, ere the bark
> of watch-dog gathers drowsy folds, to shed
> A sister's tears. Kind Heaven, upon her head,
> Do thou in dove-like guise thy spirits pour,
> And in her aged path some flowerets spread
> Of earthly joy, should time for her in store
> Have weary days and nights, ere she shall greet
> Him whom she longs in Paradise to meet.

Only Robert Southey recognised the reality of the Lambs' relationship, that the weight of need had always been heaviest on Charles's side. 'Forlorn as his poor sister will feel herself,' he wrote, 'it is better that she should be the survivor. Her happiness, such as it was, depended less upon him than his upon her.'

Mary was a survivor. Only three out of the seven Lamb children had reached adulthood and she, in so many ways the weakest of that trio, proved herself to be the toughest and outlasted them all. Once again, she rallied and, by March, she was sane. Now she felt the full force of her loss but she did not cry, just moaned sadly when she talked of her brother. Her friends wanted her to leave the Waldens immediately. They wrote letters to each other urging Mary's immediate removal from Edmonton. 'The people appear very attentive to her, but I should prefer her living with Miss James if that could be arranged hereafter,' wrote Talfourd to Crabb Robinson. And, again, a few months later,

'I cannot bear the thought of her remaining unsolaced and alone, as she must feel herself, now she is capable of feeling like herself, and besides difficulties in removing her may arise if she should relapse and the coarse-minded people she is with should influence her to fancy she would rather remain with them.' Mary was stubborn and strong-minded enough to resist. For a while, she wanted – needed – to be near Charles's grave, she 'used, when well, to stroll out mournfully in the evening, and to this spot she would contrive to lead any friend who came in the summer evenings to drink tea and went out with her afterwards for a walk'. Locals remembered her wandering the streets of Edmonton, a dotty but determined old lady, asking strangers about her brother.

Meanwhile, those friends were also busy with the grand literary project of writing and publishing the biography of Charles, and her presence was something of a hindrance to them. She objected to Wordsworth's poem 'Written After the Death of Charles Lamb', which was originally intended to be an epitaph for his headstone. She took exception to the reference to her brother as a clerk – 'to the strict labours of the merchant's desk / By duty chained' and to the suggestions

Edmonton.

of problems – 'troubles strange / many and strange that hung about his life'. Robinson excused her to Wordsworth, 'Dear Mary with all her excellences is not without a tinge of vanity. She does not take pleasure in seeing the *servile* state and humble life of her brother recorded. And she shrinks naturally enough from all allusion to calamities or sufferings.' Dear Mary might have been seventy years old and out of her mind half the time but she still had enough spirit to take issue with the great Wordsworth's verse. She thought highly of her brother's work, she had often been his muse as well as his first critic, she knew the care and trouble he had taken with his writing; to her he was a writer first and an office worker second. She probably disliked the reference to Charles as the 'the most gentle Creature nursed in fields', knowing how it would have exasperated her often waspish brother. She might too have preferred a total silence on the subject of suffering to Wordsworth's hints.

Edward Moxon, the husband of Emma Isola, commissioned the first biography of Charles Lamb. Talfourd, Charles's old friend was entrusted with the project. He had known both Mary and Charles since 1815. At the time of their meeting, Mary had been fifty-one, Charles forty and Talfourd only twenty. He had been a youthful admirer of the older man's writings. He thought still more of the man, naming one of his sons after him. He had reviewed his work and drunk his beer and was one of the executors of Charles's will. His parents had cared for Mary in their madhouse in Fulham. He sat firmly on the inner rung of the Lambs' circle of friends. There were dissenters – Charles's friend, Barron Field thought Talfourd had 'too much to do and would write too fine' – but most of Lambs' circle had agreed that he was the right man for the job. All Charles's friends were prepared to share anecdotes, reminiscences and allow letters to be published. Even in a period where biography often approached hagiography, this was a particularly intimate, close-knit project. The writer, publisher and contributors were all close to the subject and, more importantly, to the subject's still-living sister. They were all agreed that Mary had to be protected from exposure.

Talfourd had had tricky commissions before. He had written a memoir of the Gothic novelist Mrs Radcliffe despite the fact that her widower cried whenever his wife's name was mentioned, even though he had swiftly consoled himself with a subsequent marriage to his housekeeper. But the thorny problem of how to tell the full story of Charles without explaining that Charles's sister had killed their mother was a tougher challenge. The right time had not come for a full biography; everyone was agreed on that. Charles's letters were 'delightful', noted Henry Crabb Robinson but 'A regard to living friends will render many suppressions necessary.'

Talfourd tackled the problem by not mentioning it. His book, *The Letters of Charles Lamb, with a Sketch of his Life*, appeared in 1837. It was dedicated to Mary Lamb and described as the 'memorials of many years which she spent with the writer in undivided affection, of the sorrows and the joys she shared, of the genius which she cherished, and of the excellences which she best knew'. At the time of the book's appearance, Mary was again mad, much too ill to read anything. Otherwise, she would have noticed – and no doubt appreciated – that Talfourd's biography was a masterpiece of editorial reticence and sympathetic discretion.

Talfourd himself in his Preface to the *Letters* declared the incompleteness of his work. 'The recentness of the period of some of the letters has rendered it necessary to omit many portions of them, in which the humour and beauty are interwoven with personal references, which, although wholly free from anything which, rightly understood, could give pain to any human being, touch on subjects too sacred for public exposure.' He was full of promises, almost teasing: 'Many letters yet remain unpublished, which will further illustrate the character of Mr Lamb, but which must be reserved for a future time, when the Editor hopes to do more justice to his own sense of the genius and the excellence of his friend.'

Given that Talfourd believed that only in knowing every-thing about Mary could the real merits of Charles be under-stood, his reticence was marvellous indeed. No modern biographer would ever be so discreet. Robert Southey thought the need for silence spoiled what could have been a fine book. 'If the whole story could have been told,' he wrote, 'this would have been one of the most painfully interesting books that ever came from the press. When I saw Talfourd last, he seemed fully aware how much better it would have been to have delayed the publication for some years. But in this age, when a person of any notoriety dies, they lose as little time in making a book of him as they used to do in making a mummy.' For other friends of Lamb's, the silence at the heart of the first biography, what it didn't say, became the hallmark of its merit. Writing on the book, Henry Crabb Robinson singled out Talfourd's reticence for particular praise. 'Talfourd,' he noted in his diary, 'has showed great judgment in the veil he has thrown over what ought not to be too palpable and intelligible.'

Meanwhile, the object of all this care and discretion lived on in Edmonton. She was ill more often than not – in 1839, for example, she was out of her mind for ten long months – but, in her rare periods of lucidity, she read French novels, received her guests graciously, chatted, played cards and walked with them to Charles's grave. Insane she certainly was but she was still able to seize such pleasures as were offered her. Crabb Robinson was particularly loyal; he found seeing her painful but he never deserted her and listened, with the best patience he could manage, to her meaningless, hard-to-understand monologues. Now that her brother was gone, there was no-one to appreciate her 'rambling chat'.

She found the people she lived with – the Waldens – disagree-able but she liked the children and stayed in Edmonton until

1841 when it became apparent to everyone that another arrangement would have to be made. Mrs Walden's temper had become so 'evil', so bad it was almost like a 'disease' she said. Mary was being neglected and the rows in the house made her excited and more prone to become ill. She wanted to live with Miss James.

And so Mary, now seventy-seven, went to live in St John's Wood, not actually with Miss James but with her old nurse's married sister, Mrs Parsons. She was a nurse too and a kind woman and, according to her nephew John Hollingshead, she fitted Mary up with a 'comfortable library sitting-room on the ground floor with a French window opening into a garden. The garden was almost an orchard – part of the great orchard which probably gave its name to Orchard Street – and this was full of trees that produced the finest apples – now all but extinct – known as ribstone Pippins.' Hollingshead recalled visits there, an afternoon spent with Mary, now a 'dreamy old lady, who looked over me rather than at me, and seemed to see many visions that were beyond my limited intelligence'. She played cards with him and let him look at her brother Charles's books that lined every wall of her room. 'Most of them were author's copies,' he remembered. 'Simply bound in rough paper or boards, with ragged-edged leaves and ample margins. They were fifty years in advance of the modern artistic publisher. Many of the folios were there that had been bought by Charles Lamb in his roamings, and brought home and carefully collated with his sister, by the aid of a tallow candle. The old dramatists were, of course, well represented, and the picaresco school of fiction, notably *The Rogue; or the Adventures of Don Gusman D'Alfarache*.' Always indulgent to young people, Mary let Hollingshead take a pinch of snuff out of a box marked with her initials.

Mary loved her new home. In one of the last of her letters,

she wrote to Jane Norris, the daughter of her old Temple friend Randal, 'I long to shew you what a nice snug place I have got into – in the midst of a pleasant little garden. I have a room for myself and my old books on the ground floor and a little bedroom up two pairs of stairs.' Best of all, she was 'in the midst of many friends'.

'When you come to town,' she went on, 'if you have not time to go to the Moxons, an omnibus from the Bell and Crown in Holborn would bring you to our door in a quarter of an hour. If your dear Mother does not venture so far, I will contrive to pop down to see her.'

She was always ready and willing 'to pop down' to see anyone. Old habits die hard; she still went out a lot – 'too much' according to Crabb Robinson. As always she lived two lives – one in the shadows where no one else went, spending days, weeks, months lost to reason, wandering the strange bewildering maze of her own mind. The other was in her snug sitting room surrounded by her brother's books or seated at a friend's dinner table. She spent evenings at Emma and Edward Moxon's parties, she visited Henry Crabb Robinson, she enjoyed a drive out with Mrs Talfourd, Miss Kelly came to call.

Her last piece of correspondence, written by Miss James on her behalf, was a sympathy note to an old friend who had lost her mother. 'She was much shocked on reading of her death, and appeared very vexed that she had not been to see her, and wanted very much to come down and see you both; but we were really afraid to let her take the journey.' The postscript implored: 'Pray don't invite her to come down to see you.' She was obviously still keen to pay visits even when they were beyond her strength. According to William Carew Hazlitt, the grandson of her old friend Sarah, she added mild kleptomania to her body of mental disturbances and took to wrapping small items up in a handkerchief and taking them away with her. Perhaps she was never quite convinced that she didn't need to worry about money.

She became severely deaf. In 1843, Crabb Robinson wrote that she was 'a mere wreck of herself'. The following year, she dislocated her shoulder, probably while struggling in a strait-jacket during a manic phase. The accident 'brought her to herself sooner than would have been,' said Crabb Robinson. Conversation with her was difficult. Not only was she deaf but she could barely speak clearly any more and her chat about acquaintances was, depressingly, 'a discourse about the dead'. For Mary had outlived most of her closest friends and acquain-tances. William Godwin, who had published her books, had died in 1836; Barron Field, who had taken a trip down memory lane with her to Mackery End, had died the year before. Hazlitt was dead and so too was her great friend Sarah Stoddart. The friends who visited her now, fond though she was of them and they of her, were friends formed in middle age, men who were much younger than she was. Her life now was like a fulfilment of the poem her brother wrote the year after her mother's death:

> Am left with a few friends, and one above
> The rest, found faithful in a length of years,
> Contented as I may, to bear me on
> To the not unpeaceful evening of a day
> Made black by morning storms.

On 20 May 1847 Mary died. She was eighty-two. It had been a long life and a tough one. Her funeral eight days later was 'a painfully interesting day' according to Crabb Robinson. On the oppressively hot afternoon, two carriages of friends including Crabb Robinson, Talfourd, Moxon and Martin

Burney accompanied Mary Lamb to her last home, the Edmonton graveyard where her brother was buried. His grave was dug open to receive her coffin. Talfourd recalled the scene in deliciously Gothic, creepily erotic prose:

> So dry . . . is the soil of the quiet churchyard that the excavated earth left perfect walls of stiff clay, and permitted us just to catch a glimpse of the still untarnished edges of the coffin in which all the mortal part of one of the most delightful persons who ever lived was contained, and on which the remains of her he had loved with love 'passing the love of woman', were henceforth to rest; – the last glances we shall ever have even of that covering; – concealed from us as we parted, by the coffin of his sister. We felt, I believe after a moment's strange shuddering, that the re-union was well accomplished.

Martin Burney annoyed the men by crying stormily but, among the others, 'no sadness was assumed' according to Crabb Robinson. 'We all felt her departure was a relief,' he said.

Afterword

Their lives should be written together.
Barron Field, 1847

SIX DAYS AFTER MARY'S funeral, Henry Crabb Robinson noted: 'Talfourd, it is understood, will now relate the whole history of the death of her mother. The second edition of the Letters will be a very valuable book.'

Talfourd's new biography, called *Final Memorials*, appeared in 1848. The Preface referred the reader back to the original biography and the reference 'to letters yet remaining unpublished', and recalled a promise that one day 'a more complete estimate might be formed of the singular and delightful character of the writer'. That day had now come, 'the dismissal of the last, and to him the dearest of all, his sister, while it has brought to her the repose she sighed for ever since she lost him, has released his biographer from a difficulty which has hitherto prevented a due appreciation of some of his noblest qualities'.

Talfourd had waited thirteen years to tell the full story of Charles Lamb. By revealing the secret of Mary's life, he felt he would be, by extension, telling the story of Charles. Talfourd placed Mary's madness early in this new version of Charles's life, in the second chapter. He also made it central to Charles's personality and his art. Out of Mary's psychodrama sprang the good and loving Charles Lamb, saintly and heroic in his self-sacrifice. His personality was formed by her illness, his gentleness by her violence, his goodness by her crime. Her helplessness provoked his loving service, her life-long neediness created his lifetime of service. His 'frailties' were linked to her mental state. His – as Talfourd now felt free to reveal – fondness for strong drink could be entirely explained and exonerated by the hardship of his life. 'Will any one, acquainted with these secret passages of Lamb's history, wonder that, with a strong physical inclination for the stimulus and support of strong drinks – which man is framed moderately to rejoice in – he should snatch some wild pleasure "between the acts" (as he called them) "of his distressful drama".'

His religious views were, according to Talfourd, shaped by *her* experiences. 'The truth is, not that he became an unbeliever, or even a sceptic, but that the peculiar disaster in which he was plunged, and the tendency of his nature to seek immediate solaces, induced an habitual reluctance to look boldly out into futurity.'

The oddities of his behaviour – 'the eccentric wildness of his mirth, his violent changes from the serious to the farcical' (which he used to such good effect in his Elia essays) – were traced to Mary. He carried within himself 'the seeds' of his sister's malady but, in his case, 'moral courage' controlled the disease, the 'power of a virtuous . . . wish' conquered the 'fiery suggestions of latent insanity'. To Talfourd, Mary's madness was the fully-fledged version of Charles' eccentricity.

Final Memorials was a success. The Lambs' friends loved it. 'I have read them through with an enjoyment not weakened but chastised by tender recollections,' Henry Crabb Robinson wrote to Talfourd; 'You have succeeded in what was a hazardous undertaking.' He thought the new letters provided 'an apology for all one wishes away in his delightful works'. Charles's boyhood friend, Valentine le Grice was deeply moved by a description of Charles and Mary on the way to an asylum: 'In the space of a few lines – a shiver came over me, and then slow burning tears – a Vibration has been given to my heart-strings which will never cease; it will never be stilled. Thank God that you have lived to record it – there is nothing like it in the history of man.'

The book was well reviewed. Thomas de Quincey thought that where Charles's character was concerned he 'gladly adopted the eloquent words of Sergeant Talfourd'. And an American reviewer thought Lamb had been 'fortunate' in his biographer. Talfourd was fitted 'to realise the intrinsic worth' of Lamb and did the job, 'with the reverence, affection, and delicacy' required for such a task.

Talfourd thought highly of his own work. 'The story of the lives of Charles and Mary Lamb is now told,' he asserted with a confidence that a modern-day biographer, plagued as they are with doubts about truth and finality, might envy. And although in term of facts and information, history has disagreed with his statement that 'nothing more remains to be learned', Talfourd's *Final Memorials* did set a precedent in conflating the life stories of Mary and Charles into joint biographies of the Lambs. 'In death they are not divided,' writes Talfourd and, down the years, successive biographers have seen the lives in terms of togetherness. Her madness the cause, his devotion the sacrifice, the ultimate result, their above average closeness. Bryan Waller Proctor introduced his 1866 biography by stating that the 'one grand and tender purpose' of Charles's life was 'to protect and save' his sister. 'Out of the misery and deso-lation caused by her madness sprang that wonderful love between brother and sister, which has no parallel in history.'

Wordsworth too helped construct this unified image of the Lambs. Another version of 'Written After the Death of Charles Lamb', called them '. . . a double tree / With two collateral stems sprung from one root' and also like 'two vessels launched / From the same beach one ocean to explore.'

Yet, in presenting a unified front of perfect togetherness, Talfourd, Proctor and Wordsworth were forced to edit out any facts that contradicted this view. Wordsworth, in particular, saw the Lambs' life through the prism created by his own experience of an intense and life-long relationship with his own sister. The truth is the Lambs had not chosen to live like this; they were making the best of a bad job. That it was a very good best does not change the fact that they sometimes struggled with and against it. Charles was often, understandably, far from cheerful about his hard duty; he knew deep depression and often despaired of the hopelessness of his life. Nor did he entirely give up hope of other loves. And Mary, though she never expected to marry and have children, certainly understood enough and thought enough of love and lovers to appreciate what she was missing.

A quarter of Mary's life was lived without her brother. She was eleven when he was born and survived him by more than a decade. And she had experiences that he could not, nor would have wanted, to share. Because of her madness and the need for incarceration, she frequently lived apart from him. Reading Mary's own words, we find a woman who led her own life, thought her own thoughts and enjoyed secrets that she kept from him. She had ideas that she shared with her female friends and not with him. She had too her own creative struggles and her own dreams of love and marriage.

The understanding Wordsworth had for deep sibling affection also prevented him from recognising the differences between his case and the Lambs. And Talfourd and Cornwall cared deeply for both Mary and Charles and wanted, like all the Lambs' friends, to search out and celebrate the silver lining in the cloud of violence and insanity that hung over their heads. And there is silver there but it is not to be found, at least not entirely, in the Lambs' ersatz marriage, nor in Charles's heroic self-sacrifice. What moves us in the lives of Mary and Charles Lamb is the hard work they both put into not being defeated by the painful circumstances of their lives. No wonder they liked playing cards so much; their whole life was a gamble against the odds. Fate dealt them – Mary in particular – a terrible hand and yet they played – they were forever playing – their cards, with grace and considerable success. Through love and loyalty, through writing and good friendships, they encountered the great tear that madness made in the fabric of their lives and repaired and repatched until it was almost as good as new.

A large headstone surrounded by railings now marks the spot in Edmonton churchyard where Mary Lamb's body lies buried on top of her brother's. He is commemorated with a sonnet, she is 'Also Mary Anne Lamb' and the inscription gets the year of her birth wrong. But she was more than just an 'also'. There was a rare and lovely gift in the shy neglected little girl who wandered through the marble halls of a mansion that didn't belong to her. Deep within her heart, she kept alive the dreams of childhood only to create them anew in fiction. There was a rare courage too. Again and again, she rose above the great tragedy of her life to find and to give pleasure.

Mary presents herself in a series of powerful images. There is the child Mary, a bookish neglected child, the teenage Mary holding her little brother by the hand. There is Mary the writer, drawing deep into the wells of her imagination to write her clever little books. And the kindly middle-aged lady who taught Latin to small boys and gave young girls the chance to gossip alone in peace. Then too there is mad Mary, her mind spinning out of control and her lips spluttering with jokes and witticisms. And my personal favourite – merry Mary, emerging from under the shadow of madness, gallivanting her way around Regency London, living out her life brightly and bravely.

List of Illustrations

Acknowledgements

A thousand thanks are due to all the wonderful people at Bloomsbury and Tarcher and to Patrick, my lovely agent. I also owe a debt of gratitude to Simeon Shoul who read the first draft and asked all the right questions and to Duncan Wu who advised me to 'dump the myth'.

A NOTE ON THE AUTHOR

The daughter of a Scottish mother and a Jamaican father, Kathy Watson was brought up in Devon. After graduating from Oxford University, she worked for the BBC and then as a journalist and editor in national women's magazines. Her first book, *The Crossing*, also a biography, was published in 2000. She is currently a freelance journalist and lives in north London with her husband and two small children.

A NOTE ON THE TYPE

The text of this book is set in Linotype Sabon, named
after the type founder, Jacques Sabon. It was designed by
Jan Tschichold and jointly developed by Linotype,
Monotype, and Stempel, in response to a need for a
typeface to be available in identical form for mechanical
hot metal composition and hand composition using
foundry type. Tschichold based his design for Sabon
roman on a font engraved by Garamond, and Sabon
italic on a font by Granjon. It was first used in 1966
and has proved an enduring modern classic.